A STRAIGHTFORWARD GUIDE TO BUYING A FRANCHISE

CHANGING YOUR LIFE WITH A BUSINESS THAT IS RIGHT FOR YOU

Gordon Clark

Straightforward Guides
© Copyright Straightforward Publishing 2015

1st Edition

ISBN:
978-1-847165-01-5

Cover design by Bookworks Islington
Printed by 4edge Ltd www.4edge.co.uk

Whilst every care has been taken to ensure the accuracy of this work, the
author or publisher cannot accept responsibility for loss occasioned by any
person acting or refraining to act as a result of any statement contained
within this book.

Contents

Introduction   11

The British Franchising Association (BFA)   11

Part 1. Franchising generally

Ch.1 What is franchising?   19

Franchising-a definition and history   19
What is business franchising?   20
Business Format Franchising   20
Product and Trade Name Franchising   21
A brief history   21
The growth of franchising   22
Franchising sectors   23
Main points from Chapter 1   26

Ch.2 Considering the good and bad points-is   27
franchising the right way to go for you?

Different aspects of franchising   27
The pro's and con's of franchising   27
PROS of franchising   28
The use of a recognisable brand   28
Ongoing support   28
Lucrative locations   28
Established market   29
Easier access to finance   29
CONS of franchising   29

Considerable costs 29

Lack of control 30

External factors 30

Discipline 30

Franchisor Monitoring 30

Service Charges 30

Reputation 31

Inflexibility 31

Responding to the market 31

The job itself 31

Finally-considerable work 31

Other risks associated with franchisor performance 32

The established franchisor 32

The new franchisor 32

Unethical franchisors 32

Incompetent franchisors 33

Are you suited to running a franchise? 34

Main points from Chapter 2 35

Ch.3 What type of franchise to choose? 37

Automotive and car repair franchises 37

Care service providers 39

Cleaning services 40

Estate agencies 41

Financial services 41

Gift cards 42

Internet franchises 43

Parcel Couriering 43

Plumbing 44

Print shops 44

Recruitment 45

Retail 46

Buying an existing franchise as opposed to a new   47
franchise
Advantages of an Existing Franchise   47
Track Record   47
Customer Base   48
Flexibility   48
Advantages of a New Franchise   48
Clean Slate   48
Lower Purchase Price   49
Newer Equipment and Facilities   49
Main points from Chapter 3   50

Ch.4 Searching for the right franchise and asking the   51
     right questions.

Where can you find details of franchises for sale?   51
Questions to ask franchisors   53
Main points from Chapter 4   55

Ch.5 Financing a franchise and preparing a business   57
     plan

Raising finance for a franchise   57
Approaching banks for finance   57
The person - Who are they lending the money to?   58
The amount - How much are you looking to borrow?   58
How do you intend to pay back the money?   59
How much risk is involved?   59
The calculation of interest and fees   59
Forms of finance   60
Total cost of opening a franchise   60
Franchise deposits   61
Franchise Fees-Initial franchise fees   62

On-going franchise fees   62
Advertising Fee   63
Franchise Business Plan   64
Preparing a business plan   64
Introduction   64
The Product or Service   65
The Personnel   65
The Market   66
The Marketing Plan   66
The Operation   67
The Premises   67
Financial Information   68
Introduction   68
Profit & Loss Forecast   68
Cash Flow Forecast   69
Appendix   69
Verifying a franchisor's projections   70
Main points from Chapter 5   72

Ch.6 the legal agreement   73

The franchise agreement   73
What is the Franchise Agreement?   73
The Terms of the agreement   73
What should I look for in a franchise agreement?   74
The Intellectual Property   75
Trade Marks and Service Marks   75
The Rules   76
Main points from Chapter 6   78

Ch.7 The franchisor's operating manual and   79
       franchisor's training

About the company   79
Support   79
Launch timetable   80
Training   80
Recruiting staff   80
Office   80
Office maintenance   80
Office Administration   80
Reporting   80
Vehicle administration   80
Marketing   80
Pricing   81
Sales Insurance   81
Corporate structure   81
Financing   81
Company   81
Field operations   81
Resale, transfer, renewal and closing   81
Expansion and relocation   81
Franchise support   81
Franchise training   83
Main points from Chapter 7   85

Ch.8 The ongoing management of your business   87

The initial phase of the business   87
Finding premises   87
Buying equipment   88
Recruiting staff   88
Employing People   88
What are my responsibilities as an employer?   89
Discrimination and the law   89
Main points from Chapter 8   91

Part 2. Basic Tips On Running Your Business-Financial Control-Products And Markets And Marketing Generally

Ch.9 Financial control   95

Financial Control   95
Profit and loss forecasting   95
Cashflow forecast   96
Preparing a Cashflow Forecast   96
Other Terms   96
Over-trading   97
Check your customer's ability to pay   97
Set out your terms of trading   97
Set up a system   98
Keep clear and accurate records   98
Collect your payment on time   98
The advantages of a bookkeeping system   99
How to record the information you need   100
Proprietary systems.   100
The Analysed Cash book System   101
The Double Entry System   102
Computerised Accounting Systems   103
Main points from Chapter 9   104

Ch.10 Products, markets and pricing   105

Segmenting the market place   105
Geographic segmentation   106
Demographic segmentation   106

Occupation and social class   106
ACORN   107
Product segmentation   107
Benefit and lifestyle segmentation   107
Competitive advantage   107
Unique selling points (USP)   109
Pricing Your Product   110
Your Costs   110
Competitors Prices   112
Main points from Chapter 10   115

Ch.11 Marketing generally   117

Market Research   117
Bringing people's attention to your product   120
Advertising   121
Leaflets   121
Directories   122
Advertising in magazines   122
Newspaper advertising   123
Television advertising   123
Radio advertising   123
Using an advertising agent   123
Direct mail   124
Using sales representatives or agents   124
Internet Marketing   125
Search engine optimization   125
Making your site visible to search engines   125
Quality content   126
The use of key words and phrases   126
Search engine marketing   127
Purchasing traffic   128
Email marketing   129

Affiliation (as advertiser)   129
Using vouchers and coupons   130
Co-registration   130
Rich media   131
Social media   131
Blogging   131
Market places   132
Main points from Chapter 11   133

Ch.12 Growing your franchise-a few tips   135

Managing staff   135
Networking   136
Knowing yourself   136
Managing time   137

Summary of the book
Glossary of terms
Useful addresses and websites

Index

****

Introduction

Over the last 30 years the franchising industry has grown enormously and, in many cases, has provided people with a lot of enjoyment and a lucrative income. I say 'most cases' because as with everything stories are legion of people getting ripped off and losing their shirt on failed ventures.

If you look at the trade papers, such as Daltons Weekly, you will see literally hundreds of franchise opportunities available. Most are tried and tested. A lot, however, are nothing short of comical, put together by people who have causally started a business, split it into 'territories' and sold the rights to trade in an area. Quite often the product or service that is being sold is spurious and bound to fail. You will see as we go through the book that it is crucial that the business that you are thinking of buying into is a member of the British Franchising Association. Right at the outset, we will discuss the bfa as it will be crucial to you if you are thinking of getting involved with franchising.

The below will give you some idea of what the bfa is and how it operates and different levels of membership and the criteria applied by the bfa.

The British Franchising Association (BFA)

Below is a statement from the BFA website:

" The British Franchise Association (bfa) is the only voluntary self-regulatory body for the UK franchise industry, with a standards based approach to membership. Its aim is to promote ethical franchising practice in the UK and help the industry develop credibility, influence and favourable circumstance for growth. As a result one of the bfa's main jobs is to help potential franchisees recognise the good, the bad, and the ugly franchise opportunities for what they are.

Another is to help to secure their own position amongst the "good" franchises".

As I mentioned earlier, there are many franchise opportunities which can turn into nightmares. Hence the existence of the bfa to act as a regulatory body.

About the bfa

In 1977 the major franchise companies in the UK decided to set up their own association. The British Franchise Association (bfa), was formed to act in the interests of the industry as a whole in assessing and accrediting franchises, the terms of the contract between franchisor and franchisee, the testing of the system and its success as a franchise. Franchisors and professional advisors to the UK franchise industry wishing to be accredited must put themselves forward to the bfa to be tested against its strict and extensive criteria. Only if they successfully pass accreditation are they then able to gain membership of the bfa, gain access to the benefits of membership and become represented by the British Franchise Association.

The role of the bfa

The British Franchise Association is the voice of ethical franchising in the UK. It is the Trade Association for those who pass accreditation and also plays a key role as educator to the many potential individuals and businesses that consider franchising. Therefore, it is very powerful and if you are considering taking on a franchise then the bfa will play a key role in your decision, or should play a key role. In recent years, the bfa has developed to include work around the engagement of franchisees into the Association and it has developed awareness campaigns to consumers and has launched industry recognised qualifications in the shape of the Qualified Franchise Professional. Details of this and other initiatives can be found on their website www.thebfa.org.

Criteria and checklist for membership

When they join the British Franchise Association members have to commit themselves to comply with the terms of the policies and procedures published by the Association. These are The Code of Ethical Conduct, The Disciplinary Procedure, The Complaints Procedure and The Appeals Procedure. Members also agree to comply with the Code of Advertising Practice as published by the Advertising Standards Authority and to abide by other regulations published on the bfa website. The following represents different types of membership. For costs of membership you should go to the bfa website..

Full and Associate Members

All Full and Associate members of the bfa must meet four key criteria: that the business is viable, franchisable, ethical and fully disclosed. With these checks in place, franchisors can be admitted to membership, providing also that they commit themselves to abide by the Advertising Standards Authority's code of practice and also to the Association's own complaints and disciplinary, appeals and re-accreditation rules. Full members will have a proven trading and franchising record. The length of time a franchised business has been in operation, and the changes in business and financial circumstances it must have survived before it can be said to be "established", will vary from sector to sector.

Provisional listing

Provisional Listing is available to businesses with a successful trading record of at least one year and that are in the process of developing a franchised business (most often with a pilot operation at this stage, whether franchised or company owned). The business will have offer documents that are free of ambiguity and misleading statements, and any direct or indirect references to future trading potential will be objective and based on actual experience. They will already have a franchise agreement that meets the bfa's Code of Ethics and will be able to demonstrate that their development programme is founded on good franchising practice. Provisionally Listed companies commit to complying with the conditions of membership and to work to achieving the standards for Associate Membership within two years.

Professional Affiliation

Professional Affiliation to the bfa is open to professional advisors who have been accredited on the basis of their proven professional skills and the successful application of those skills to franchising. They undertake to ensure that the advice on franchising that they provide to clients is of a standard consistent with the aims and objectives of the European Code of Ethics. The involvement of bfa affiliated advisors in the development of franchise companies is one of the measures the bfa uses in assessing companies for Provisional Listing. Affiliate membership is limited to six core discipline areas, Finance (banks and accountants) Legal, Franchise consultants (business development), Franchise consultants (recruitment and brokers) Recruitment media – websites, recruitment media – magazines and newspapers

As you have seen, it is crucial that if you are thinking about getting involved in the world of franchising, the first step should be to consult the bfa. Although not everyone is a member, if they are then this will give you the security to want to pursue your particular business option as the business will have passed through many rigorous tests to arrive at their membership..

It is the express intention of this book to guide people through the process of purchasing and developing a successful franchise. Franchising and the history of franchising is explained. The nature and types of franchises available, plus the various business models is also explained. Following this the all-important area of franchise finance is discussed in depth as without adequate financing you won't go forward.

Having covered the initial steps, we will cover the legal agreements underpinning franchising and what can be expected by both franchisor (organisation or person selling the business) and franchisee (purchaser). Finally, we cover the creation of a business plan which is central to the future development of your franchise and we discuss the initial months of trading, getting the business off the ground. Then, if you are feeling adventurous we will discuss expanding your empire.

Overall, this book will prove invaluable for the would-be franchisee.

Good luck in your venture.

Gordon Clarke.

Part 1

Franchising Generally

Chapter 1

What is Franchising?

Franchising-a definition and History

The word 'franchise' is used in several contexts. In most dictionaries, the word is defined as follows:

1.
A privilege or right officially granted a person or a group by a government, especially:

a. The constitutional or statutory right to vote.
b. The establishment of a corporation's existence.
c. The granting of certain rights and powers to a corporation.
d. Legal immunity from servitude, certain burdens, or other restrictions.

2.
a. *Authorization granted to someone to sell or distribute a company's goods or services in a certain area.*
b. A business or group of businesses established or operated under such authorization.
c. A brand name under which a series of products is released.

3. The territory or limits within which immunity, a privilege, or a right may be exercised.

You can see that particularly in the second definition, at its root, 'franchise' means that a right has been granted to someone or some group to do something or to have the power to do something-such as vote. In the context of this book, we are talking about business franchising.

What is business franchising?

In simple terms, a franchise is an agreement between two parties which allows one party i.e. the franchisee, to market products or services using the trademark and operating methods of the other party i.e. the franchisor. These rights are usually granted in return for a fee.

There are two types of franchise methods - business format franchising and product and trade name franchising.

Business Format Franchising

The most common method in the UK is Business Format Franchising. Using this method, when you buy a franchise, the franchisor grants you, the franchisee, the use of their logos and trademarks, as well as a turn-key system for doing business. This includes helping the franchisee with site selection, store layout and design, recruiting and training staff, marketing the business, preferred supplies contacts and more.

The franchisee in return has to pay an upfront franchise fee as well as ongoing royalties to the franchisor. The franchisor uses this money to help further develop the system through marketing, product and market research, and ongoing support.

There are many examples of business format franchising opportunities, including – food franchises, automotive franchises, estate agency franchises, retail franchises, recruitment franchises, children's franchises, coffee franchises, pet franchises, fitness franchises, to name but a few.

Many of these are home-based franchises, part-time franchises and mobile franchises, and not all require a high level of investment, some are considered low-cost franchises. See the list of potential franchise areas at the end of this chapter.

Product and Trade Name Franchising

The other franchise method is Product and Trade Name Franchising. This type of franchising does not involve royalty fees. The most important thing that the franchisor provides to someone buying a franchise in Product and Trade Name Franchising is the product. The franchisee is required to purchase the product or range of products exclusively from the franchisor. The franchisor also provides national marketing and advertising campaigns, logos and trademarks.

This type of franchising is mainly associated with industries such as petroleum, soft drink distribution and automotive.

Product and Trade Name Franchising has three distinctive characteristics:

- The franchisee sells goods which are supplied by the franchisor or a person affiliated with the franchisor;
- The franchisor helps the franchisee to secure accounts or, depending on the type of business, locations or sites for rack displays or vending machines.
- Within 6 months of opening the business, the franchisee must pay the franchisor or a person affiliated with the franchisor

A brief history

The practice of franchising, providing a service in a specified territory for a defined fee, dates back hundreds of years, even going back as far as the middle ages. So, you won't be involved in anything new! In more recent times, the mid 1880's, the Singer Sewing Machine Company is credited with having set up the first modern franchise. Whilst the company manufactured on a mass scale, and sold its products on a mass scale it was unable to provide after care services, such as repairs and maintenance so split its sales areas into franchises and sold the rights to the brand, sales and after care to franchisees.

Other big business in the USA followed suit over time with General Motors establishing a franchise and the more obvious ones such as McDonalds, Burger King, Cocoa Cola and Pepsi Cola establishing worldwide franchises.

In the UK franchising also took off but people began to get suspicious of the practice due to its lack of regulation and the incidence of people being ripped off.

In the face of this growing concern, In 1977 as we have seen, the British Franchise Association was formed, created by the major players in the UK, such as Dyno Rod and the Wimpey Hamburger Chain. As with many trade associations, or umbrella groups, it came into existence to provide some sort of regulation in the industry. The big players were also concerned to ensure that their own business models didn't suffer and that they could continue to attract franchisee's.

The growth of franchising
It has been the case that, since the start of the current recession, franchising has out-performed other business start ups, in the main because with franchising most of the groundwork needed to set up a business has already been done and is in place. The franchisee steps into the shoes of an already successful business. You don't have to come up with a unique selling point and start marketing from scratch. Training will be available in areas that you need and, in many cases,

you will benefit from national advertising campaigns. Obviously, the bigger and more successful the brand, such as McDonalds or Subway, the more it will cost to enter the market.

Currently, there are over 40,000 franchise units in the UK. The average age of franchisees is 49, although people of all ages get involved. In reality, as long as finance is there, age is not a barrier.

Franchising sectors

If you want to get an idea of the different sectors in which there are franchise opportunities you should go to one of the main websites that have directories of franchises and also offer franchises for sale.

The best sites are:

www.franchisedirect.co.uk
www.thefranchisedirectory.net
www.franchiseinfo.co.uk

All of these sites will offer a comprehensive list of areas. In summary below are the main areas in which you will find opportunities:

- Accountancy & Financial
- Automotive & Car
- Business to Business
- Business Consulting
- Business Opportunities
- Business Training
- Care Health and Senior Care
- Children's Franchise Opportunities

- Cleaning Franchise
- Coffee
- Computers
- Couriers
- Dating
- Education
- Event and Wedding Planning
- Fitness
- Food
- Gardening
- Golf
- Health & Beauty
- Home Care
- Home Improvements
- Home Services
- Internet
- Magazine
- Merchandising
- Mortgage
- Pest Control
- Pets
- Photography
- Print & Sign
- Professional Service
- Property & Estate Agency
- Recruitment
- Retail
- Safety & Security
- Sport Franchise
- Travel & Leisure
- Vending

The list is not exhaustive. On the above mentioned websites, if you open up each sector you will see many more-sub divisions each with franchising opportunities. There will be one to suit you, no doubt. A word of warning-you will find the good, the bad and the ugly. There are many opportunities which would be a struggle. In short, franchising has become a business in itself, selling licences and making lots of money and leaving the person on the other end without adequate back up and support.

It is up to you to look deeply into a business opportunity and to see whether it is viable. Check it out with the British franchise Association. See if the franchisor is a member to begin with. You will find many really good opportunities and with hard work you can create a successful business. Avoid the areas where it is obvious, or should be obvious, that you would lose your shirt.

In the next chapter, we will look at whether franchising is right for you as an individual, whether you are suited and what qualities you need.

Now read a summary overleaf of the main points from Chapter 1.

****

Main points from Chapter 1
What is Franchising?

- The word 'franchise' is used in several contexts. At its root, 'franchise' means that a right has been granted to someone or some group to do something or to have the power to do something. In the context of this book, we are talking about business franchising.

- In simple terms, a franchise is an agreement between two parties which allows one party i.e. the franchisee, to market products or services using the trademark and operating methods of the other party i.e. the franchisor. These rights are usually granted in return for a fee.

- There are two types of franchise methods - business format franchising and product and trade name franchising.

- Currently, there are over 40,000 franchise units in the UK. The average age of franchisees is 49, although people of all ages get involved. In reality, as long as finance is there, age is not a barrier.

****

Chapter 2

Considering The Good and Bad Points-Is Franchising The Right Way to Go For You?

Different aspects of franchising

If you are considering buying a franchise then you need to raise your awareness of exactly what this entails and whether you will be suited to the lifestyle. For example, if you buy into a fast food franchise you will need to take on board the long hours that this entails. Does this fit into your current lifestyle and would you have to make radical changes to accommodate the new business?

In this chapter we will consider a number of key areas that may affect your decision to buy a franchise business: the pro's and con's of running a franchise and also the types of franchise and the advantages and disadvantages of these, what running a franchise may entail and also your own personal qualities, i.e. are you as a person cut out to manage a business?

The pro's and con's of franchising

As we have seen, many franchise models have the potential for decent returns but for sure there's a lot of hard work involved. This will differ according to the franchise of course but certainly in the early years a lot of time and effort is needed. Like all business ideas, there are pros and cons – deciding whether a franchise will work for you is essential as the start-up costs can be considerable. We will be considering finance a little later but first we should look at the for and against aspects of franchising.

PROS of franchising
The use of a recognisable brand

For sure, a recognisable and trusted brand is a very key element to business success. However, building a reputable brand takes a lot of money and years of hard work which is why it costs a significant amount of money to buy in to it. Partnering with a well-known franchisor can do some of this hard work for you. People instantly recognise the quality of the brand and you do not need to establish so much goodwill for them to buy your products or services. Having said this, you need to look carefully at the brand you are buying in to. Some franchises may have a proven business model but the brand may not yet be embedded in the public's mind.

Ongoing support

Many first time franchisees choose franchising because of the ongoing support and guidance available. There are big advantages in having regular advice to keep you going in the right direction. The level of support will vary but many franchisors will not only provide on-the-job training but also assist in lead generation, accounting and start-up costs. They may also provide assistance or support with marketing campaigns.

Lucrative locations

Because (most) franchisors have access to more finance than first time business owners, they can afford to buy property in the best locations and give your franchise the best chance of success. Even the franchisors that don't buy the property will usually assist you in purchasing in a better location, for example by negotiating with commercial lettings managers.

Established market

Those that choose to go it alone in business must spend significant amounts of time defining their market, demographic and target customer. Not only does this cost money and take skills to carry out the necessary research, but it does not guarantee sales or even interest. Franchises work with established markets where the research has already been proven effective – you go into the business knowing who you'll be selling to and where you'll be selling.

Easier access to finance

Bank managers assess loan applications on the basis of risk – the riskier the operation the less chance the bank will see a return. Since franchises work with proven business models and often have the backing of a large parent company, banks are more likely to lend to franchises than independent businesses.

CONS of franchising
Considerable costs

Franchises can be very expensive. Franchisors typically charge an initial lump sum 'joining fee,' which can range from under a thousand pounds to tens of thousands depending on what is included. If equipment and materials are not included, you may have to purchase these separately. You'll also have to pay royalties to the franchisor, typically a percentage based on your turnover, as well as standard business overheads which can really stretch your budget. Once your franchise agreement comes up for renewal, you may need to pay a one-off cost to extend it; this will depend on the franchisor.

Lack of control

Franchise agreements will make it very clear what you can and can't do – contract breaches can result in termination of the franchise without repayment of funds invested. Franchisors generally do not like divergence from the brand so you'll likely be told precisely how to set up your premises and will have little say in how things are structured. The way you generate leads may also be subject to scrutiny.

External factors

Many things can affect the success of your business, even those that are outside of your control. With franchises not limited geographically, another franchisee may start operating in your area and push you out due to increased cash flow or shrewder practices. If this is legitimate under the terms of your franchise agreement, there's nothing you can do about it. Likewise, poor decisions by the franchisor may seriously affect business – if their brand suffers then you may start losing customers.

Discipline: Buying (licensing) a franchise means working within a system in which there is little freedom or scope to be creative. Almost every aspect of operating the business is laid down in the manuals.

Franchisor Monitoring: Regular field staff monitoring visits are welcome initially, but as time passes you will feel able to do your own trouble-shooting and you may come to regard the franchisors interest as an intrusion - it is after all your business.

Service Charges: At first these services are necessary and franchisees do not mind paying for them. However as time goes on, if less use is made of the franchisors services then franchisees can resent making the continuing payments.

Reputation: Each franchisee affects the reputation of the whole system depending on their performance and ability. In many franchises there is a wide gulf in the quality of product or service between the best and the worst franchisees. Thus any franchisee can harm the reputation of all outlets in the chain, even internationally.

Inflexibility

Responding to the market: Franchising tends to be an inflexible method of doing business as each franchisee is bound by the franchise contract to operate the business format in a certain way. This can make it difficult for a franchisor to introduce changes to the business format, refit outlets, or introduce new types of equipment. In some franchises it can be difficult for a franchisee to respond to new competition or to a change in the local market.

The job itself: What may seem an attractive challenge now could become boring after a few years, so it is important that you choose a franchise to buy in which you will enjoy the work, or which has potential for growth.

Finally-considerable work

Franchises take enormous amounts of effort to get off the ground. Although the franchisor does provide initial support, this is merely a helping hand – it's down to you to get the business running profitably. You'll need to implement the chosen business model and then hone it to work effectively within the context of your working environment, staff members and experience.

Other risks associated with franchisor performance

It is important to recognise that not all franchise businesses are soundly based or well run. In signing the franchise agreement you are formally binding yourself to a particular franchisor and it is therefore vital to select one which is competent and ethical. It has been identified that there are different categories of franchisor: established; new; unethical and incompetent. Obviously, some should be avoided at all costs and others will differ in attractiveness according to the level of risk you are prepared to take.

The established franchisor

This represents the least risky type of franchise opportunity. The business format will have been fully tested in a number of locations, most likely abroad too, and although the initial cost of opening such a franchise may be relatively high, a franchise with this type of company will be highly attractive to anyone for whom security is important.

The new franchisor

There is nothing intrinsically wrong with a new franchise but great care must be taken when deciding to invest in any particular franchise. As franchisors incur high initial costs, they need a minimum number of franchises to break even. When a franchisor has fewer than the break-even number of franchises it is likely that more effort will go into selling franchises than into providing support services. There will usually be some deficiencies in services in order to keep costs down.

Unethical franchisors

Unfortunately some franchisors have no intention of entering a long-term support relationship with the franchisee, instead they have heard that franchising is a way to make money quickly out of gullible franchisees. This is done by setting up a shell franchise - lots on offer but nothing to back it up, then selling such franchises to those who are so keen to become a franchisee that they fail to make a thorough appraisal of the business on offer. Make sure that you spot this type of franchise, take time to investigate different opportunities.

Incompetent franchisors

These are franchisors who are not offering franchises to perpetrate fraud but who are incompetent in one or more of the following ways

- The basic business is unsound
- The franchisor is under-resourced and may not be able to fund the initial running of the business
- The franchisor has not run a pilot test so cannot confirm that the business is actually franchiseable
- They have not used experience or accredited franchise consultants or lawyers
- Their manuals and start-up assistance and support is of poor quality

All of the above are minefields to avoid if you want to get off to a good start. Therefore, best to do your homework and investigate the franchisor before committing. Make sure that the franchisor belongs to the bfa. If it doesn't then it will be necessary to obtain expert advice to ensure that you are protected.

You should also ask why they are not a bfa member.

Are you suited to running a franchise?

Before you start to evaluate potential franchises, you will need to assess your own strengths and weaknesses. Implementing the standard practices of your franchisor is a massive task, as is improving on them and this will take dedication and a lot of support from your family and friends. The franchisor will be looking for a certain type of person to operate their franchise and you will need to impress them.

The key attributes of a successful franchisee include:

- Passionate about the brand – with a good knowledge of the market
- Good motivator
- Possess business acumen and awareness
- Organised
- Effective time-management skills
- Articulate
- People-person
- Good listener
- Effective communicator
- Professional in outlook and appearance
- Open to advice and guidance

Key attributes evolve around the ability to take advice and guidance from others. Another key attribute is the ability to work hard in environments that very often include unsocial hours.

Now read a summary of the main points from chapter 2 overleaf.

****

Main points from Chapter 2
Considering The Good and Bad Points-Is Franchising The Right Way to Go For You?

- If you are considering buying a franchise then you need to raise your awareness of exactly what this entails and whether you will be suited to the lifestyle. For example, if you buy into a fast food franchise you will need to take on board the long hours that this entails. Does this fit into your current lifestyle and would you have to make radical changes to accommodate the new business?

- Like all business ideas, there are pros and cons – deciding whether a franchise will work for you is essential as the start-up costs can be considerable.

- It is important to recognise that not all franchise businesses are soundly based or well run. In signing the franchise agreement you are formally binding yourself to a particular franchisor and it is therefore vital to select one which is competent and ethical.

- Before you start to evaluate potential franchises, you will need to assess your own strengths and weaknesses. Implementing the standard practices of your franchisor is a massive task, as is improving on them and this will take dedication and a lot of support from your family and friends. The franchisor will be looking for a certain type of person to operate their franchise and you will need to impress them.

······················

Chapter 3

Which Type of Franchise to Choose?

The type of franchise that you buy will very much depend on what you are looking for and what you feel that you are best equipped to run. There are different types of franchise, ranging from single operator franchises where you operate the business alone with no employees (examples of these might be businesses such as snap-on tools or mobile car repair franchises) to franchises where you run a business with employees and have to provide management and support. Such franchises could be burger or sandwich outlets or mail box franchises.

There are other types of business, such as those which provide consultancy services. We will concentrate on the areas outlined to begin with, as other franchise types, such as developing a franchise in the UK on behalf of a bigger company, may not be relevant at this point.

Below, we will look at a few of the business areas available, in alphabetical order, and the skills and abilities you will need to bring to these operations.

Automotive and car repair franchises

These will usually fall into several categories. You will have seen mobile repair vans that go around repairing scratches and dents, windscreens, wheels and interiors. Basically, you would be offering a service that will require excellent customer service skills, which will enable you to build up a client base who will offer repeat business.

There are also workshop based businesses. These tend to require the skills of a mechanic. Again, like any business, good customer service is the key to success. Being part of a franchise with a big name is of course the key to success but your own presence and how you run your business is key to the whole enterprise.

One particular company offering services to the auto industry is Autosmart. This particular opportunity deals with vehicle cleaning products. This business is designed for single franchisees operating alone, operating from a mobile showroom, laid out inside like a supermarket. As well as supplying the car, bike, truck and bus sector they also supply customers such as factories, farms, caravan sites and offices. Typically it will cost a minimum of £12,000 to buy in. They can be contacted on www.startautosmart.co.uk email franchising@autosmart.co.uk.

Another well known company offering franchises is snap-on tools. This is a mobile tool store selling directly to businesses and is over 90 years old. the cost for entry here is anything between £17,960-£73,260 plus VAT depending on territory. They can be contacted through their website www.snaponfranchise.co.uk.

Below are some other websites of companies offering opportunities in the automotive sector.

http://www.etyres.co.uk/
www.puncturesafe.co.uk
www.chipsaway.co.uk
www.thewheelspecialist.co.uk
www.mrclutchfranchise.co.uk
www.vanfranchise.co.uk
franchisedirect.co.uk/automotivefranchises
www.automotivefranchise.com

There are many opportunities available in this sector and you obviously need to be a practical person, someone who is prepared to work hard and also be good with people.

Care service providers

This is an altogether different industry and the skills required from you would also be different. In the main, you would be operating an agency providing people to look after others, predominantly (although not only) older people. You would be operating a recruitment agency and would need a knowledge of legislation and the ability to keep up with the changes in legislation. You would need to have many carers on your books and would need to employ staff to run the office. You would also need excellent interpersonal skills as you would be dealing with the private and public sectors.

In short, there are a lot of responsibilities associated with this type of franchise and a lot of different skills needed. Staff recruitment and pay and ongoing training are likely to be your biggest type of expenditure. I think that it goes without saying that, although the franchisors always state that they will provide support and training, some kind of background and experience in the sector would be needed before deciding to commit yourself to a franchise.

One such company operating in this area is Clarriots care. They are a management franchise offering care services right across the sector. they were established in 2009 and it costs between £70,000-£100,000 to enter. they offer a full package of support and training. You can obtain more details through www.clarriotshomecare.co.uk.

Overleaf are the websites of some of the other companies offering care franchises.

http://enquiries.caremarkfranchises.com

http://www.bluebirdcare.co.uk
http://247phc.com
www.kareplus.co.uk/franchising

Cleaning services

There are many type of cleaning service franchises, ranging from office and home cleaning to furniture and upholstery cleaning and carpet cleaning. Most can be run from home as the staff that you hire to carry out the work will work at the premises. Most of the staff will be women so they will work part time and fit in the work around childcare.

As with all business you will need good people skills. In the case of cleaning you will need to be able to supervise and have a knowledge of finance and payment of wages and also tax management. You will also need vehicles (which can be leased). True, the franchisor will offer support and training but underlying this you will bring your own skills and experience to the job. Although cleaning may seem easy, it is like any other business and requires good all-round skills and customer care.

One such company operating in the field is Dublcheck who have been in business for 20 years and offer cleaning franchises with entry costs ranging from £10,000-£200,000 depending on territory. They offer full back up and support.

Another company is Safeclean by Guardsman who offer carpet and upholstery cleaning services to domestic and business customers. Entry level here is £15,750 and they can be contacted though their website www.safeclean.co.uk.

Overleaf are the websites of a few of the other businesses offering such franchises.

www.diamondhomessupport.com
www.janiking.com
www.totalcleanfranchise.co.uk
www.mollymaid.co.uk
www.thomascleaningfranchise.co.uk

Estate agencies

This type of franchise requires many skills and also requires some knowledge of the property industry and how it works. You would need financial skills, legal knowledge and also staff management skills and general people skills Like the care industry, it would help greatly if you had some knowledge of this particular industry.

You could also enter the business of lettings agent, quite often an estate agency would also have a lettings agent running parallel. Again, this requires specific legal skills and people skills. One such well known company operating in this area is Century 21 Estate and Letting Agency. They have been in existence for over 40 years and operate internationally. Entry level is around £50,000 and this particular company will provide a lot of support to their franchisees.

Below are the websites of some of the other companies offering such franchises:

www.ewemove.com
http://www.huntersfranchising.co.uhttp:
www.martinco.com
https://www.estatesdirect.com

Financial services

Franchises in this particular sector are usually based around business advisory services, such as advising operations how to reduce costs or save tasks, or bookkeeping and accountancy services. Like the aforementioned franchises, you will need some kind of experience in this area, certainly a head for figures, although direct financial experience may not be necessary.

One such company operating in this area is Tax Assist Accountants who offer accountancy services to individuals and business throughout the UK. They offer full training and support and you do not have to be an accountant to operate with them. Entry is from an initial £20,000 liquid capital up to a total £50,000 investment. More details through their website www.taxassistfranchise.co.uk.

Below are the websites of some of the companies offering such franchises.

www.payrolls direct
www.erafranchise.net
www.what-partnership.co.uk

Gift cards

This is an area that is generally over subscribed so it would be wise to know what you are doing before you enter into a franchise.

You might have seen the difficulties faced by such business in the face of the internet and ecards. In addition, a lot of cold calling will be required and the market is very competitive. It goes without saying that you would need sales skills to succeed in such a business. Below are the websites of a few of the business operating in this area.

www.cards-for-you.co.uk
www.card-connection.co.uk

Internet franchises

This franchise sector is very diverse and encompasses many areas from software development to web design and search marketing services. Whatever you choose you will need basic IT skills, but won't need to be an expert. Obviously, the more you know and the better you are to begin with the more this will help you.

Internet franchises may also involve selling online advertising, or may be concerned with IT consultancy or support. Franchisees buy the right to trade under the franchisors name and often operate from home so overheads are low. There are a wide range of internet franchises and the costs of getting involved will vary significantly. You will need to have good interpersonal skills as in many cases you will be out and about meeting people. Below are some of the websites of companies offering franchises.

http://franchise.spoton.net
www.eazi-apps-business.co.uk
www.theflyingdoctor.com
www.franchise.pcpal.co.uk

Parcel Couriering

These franchises will generally fall into two distinct categories: depot based franchises where you would have responsibility for vehicles, drivers and general liaison with the wider network; a courier franchise where you operate with a van and your own territory. You would normally be based at home and be out and about. The hours are long, often unsocial, whether you are in a depot or out on the road. The price of such franchises will vary with the size of the operation and the amount of equipment you have.

The skills that you would require here can be taught by the franchisors but you would need all the range of skills that are required by other business, such as people management if you are in a depot, financial management and customer service skills. Below are the websites of a few of the businesses operating in this area.

www.speedyfreight.co.uk
www.interlinkexpress.com

Plumbing

This is one area that has seen rapid growth over the years. Plumbers are in demand. In addition, you don't need to be a qualified plumber to start out, although it helps if you have some sort of experience. Franchise opportunities in this area will include training in water regulation and gas safety.

Typically, franchisees will purchase a licence for a business where they will have exclusive rights to a territory, trading under the franchisors name and benefiting from the company's training and support.

The level and size of the operation will determine the initial cost and responsibilities but once again you will need business and customer care skills in addition to practical skills. For the right person, opportunities in the area of plumbing can be very lucrative. Below are the websites of a few of the businesses operating in this area.

www.yourplumber-uk.com
www.boilergenie.com/franchise

Print shops

These franchises can be expensive and their success depends on location. Typically, franchises such as Kall Kwik or Mail

Boxes Etc operate in this area. Franchisors will be looking for potential franchisees who can demonstrate specific skills such as sales and marketing and management. As with all franchises, a knowledge of the industry would be an advantage, particularly IT knowledge as the whole industry is driven by information technology. Producing business cards and stationary is only the tip of the iceberg! Below are the websites of a few of the businesses operating in this area.

www.mbe.co.uk (Mail Boxes Etc)
www.middlemanpress.co.uk
www.kallkwik.co.uk

Recruitment

If you are thinking about investing in a franchise in this area, ideally you would be from a management or sales background. Even more ideally, you might be from a Human Resources background.

Recruitment falls into two general categories, commercial recruitment and executive recruitment, or headhunting. Commercial recruitment handles low to medium range jobs, placing employees in public sector roles such as housing or social work, to placing operatives in warehouses and any other job that needs filling for whatever reason. Commercial recruitment will involve lots of cold calling and face to face meetings, you will need business and people management skills and a knowledge of finance and tax legislation as well as employment law. Very importantly, you will need to work at building up your client base.

At the outset, setting up and expanding a business within the recruitment industry is difficult but can be rewarding. Below are the websites of a few of the businesses operating in this area.

www.redlinegroup.com
www.247professional.com
www.antalfranchising.com
www.additionalresources.net

Retail

Retail franchises cover a wide variety of areas, taking in fast food and takeaways, hairdressing, shoe repairs and curtains, among many others. Amongst the best known ones are McDonalds, Subways and Clarks shoes. As with all retail, location is the key, as you will depend on walk-in customers. The hours will be long and the skills will include business management generally. Running a McDonalds for example requires a wide range of skills, from food management to people management to financial control. It can be a headache but very rewarding. Needless to say, McDonalds franchises are expensive costing up to £325,000 but you are buying an income and must be prepared to work at it. Subway sandwiches come in at a lesser cost but the work is still long and hard and will require the same skills. Remember, the key is location. Below are the websites of a few of the many businesses operating in this area.

www.mcdonalds.co.uk/franchising
www.steaknshake.com
www.snapon.com
www.greenekingpubs.co.uk
www.marstonscareers.co.uk
www.subway.co.uk business/franchise

We have detailed some of the franchise areas in which you can operate and the costs of operation will vary, depending on what it is you are buying, where it is, and the strength of the brand you are buying into and the level of support that you get. The skills that you will need will vary depending on what it is you are entering into. Some require specific skills, such as recruitment, other skills you can pick up on the job, such as sandwich making. However, one thing all businesses have in common is that you will need basic business skills such as people management and bookkeeping plus some idea of legislation. **Customer service** is paramount. Everyone wants to feel that they are a valuable customer and that they will be treated well and that the product they receive is quality. All too many businesses fall over in this regard and lose custom because of it. A good franchisor with a strong brand will offer training and support in this area.

Buying an existing franchise as opposed to a new franchise

The key to this decision is to understand the opportunities and challenges and the fundamental differences between existing and new franchises before you make any decisions. By thoroughly evaluating the pros and cons of each approach, you can minimize the potential for nasty surprises and significantly improve the odds of success in franchising.

Advantages of an Existing Franchise

There is a general sense among buyers that acquiring an existing franchise is easier than launching a new franchise outlet. That may or may not be the case, depending on the specifics of the outlet, but it is true that existing franchises offer several advantages that are worth considering:

1. Track Record

An existing franchise opportunity can be a turnkey business acquisition. The business is already operational so the seller should be able to demonstrate a track record of profitability as well as hard numbers that will help you determine current cash flow and make better projections regarding future performance-two key elements in the value of the business.

2. Customer Base

An established and loyal customer base is a huge benefit for a new business owner. Existing franchises make it even easier for new owners to leverage the advantage of an established customer because the franchise brand gives customers a sense of consistency, even if an ownership transition has occurred behind the scenes.

3. Flexibility

Franchisors typically have a set fee structure for new franchise locations, limiting the buyer's ability to negotiate on terms or price. Buying an existing franchise, however, puts you directly across the table from the seller with more ability to negotiate the terms and maximize the return on your investment.

Advantages of a New Franchise

New franchise outlets have higher risks and, thus, potentially higher rewards. While every franchise opportunity is different, new franchisees often discover that building a new location from the ground up provides benefits that simply aren't available with an existing operation:

1. Clean Slate

A new franchise offers buyers a clean slate; a business opportunity unaffected by the habits, preferences and/or shortcomings of a previous owner. Although you'll have to work harder to establish your business in the community, you don't have to worry about the possibility of negative customer impressions haunting your business.

2. Lower Purchase Price

New franchises are often less expensive because you aren't buying existing cash flow from an established customer base and you aren't paying for "goodwill" value often expected by sellers of existing franchises. A business with a solid reputation and a strong customer following is clearly worth more than one that is just getting off the ground. If the new franchise is successful, you'll be the beneficiary of the company's goodwill value--not the seller.

3. Newer Equipment and Facilities

When you buy a new franchise, it's likely that your equipment and facilities will also be new or at least newer than they would be if you bought an existing franchise. Outdated equipment isn't always a deal-breaker, but in some sectors (e.g. food service franchising) it's important to make sure the business is outfitted with reliable machines and the latest designs.

Ultimately, the decision to buy a new or existing franchise boils down to your personality, preferences and risk threshold. In general, proven franchises are a safer investment, but if the idea of breaking ground in a new franchise area doesn't phase you (or even appeals to you), then a new franchise might be a better option.

Now read a summary of the main points from chapter 3 overleaf.

....

Main points from Chapter 3
Which Type of Franchise to Choose?

- The type of franchise that you buy will very much depend on what you are looking for and what you feel that you are best equipped to run. There are different types of franchise, ranging from single operator franchises where you operate the business alone with no employees (examples of these might be businesses such as snap-on tools or mobile car repair franchises) to franchises where you run a business with employees and have to provide management and support.

- The skills that you will need will vary depending on what it is you are entering into. Some require specific skills, such as recruitment, other skills you can pick up on the job, such as sandwich making. However, one thing all businesses have in common is that you will need basic business skills such as people management and bookkeeping plus some idea of legislation.

- Customer service is paramount. Everyone wants to feel that they are a valuable customer and that they will be treated well and that the product they receive is quality. All too many business fall over in this regard and lose custom because of it. A good franchisor with a strong brand will offer training and support in this area.

- There are pro's and con's of buying a new franchise business as opposed to an existing franchise which should be considered carefully.

....

Chapter 4

Searching For the Right Franchise and Asking The Right Questions

---

Where can you find details of franchises for sale?

If you want to start a franchise, or are thinking of doing so, the first thing to do is to contact the franchisor direct. There are a number of ways to do this, the most convenient being the internet. As mentioned in the previous chapters, there are numerous sites with details of those companies that offer franchises. Many of the best known brands don't need to advertise that heavily as they will receive many enquiries directly from the public. They then filter out the interested parties and decide who might be suitable for their franchise opportunities.

Below are some of the best known websites listing franchise opportunities:

www.franchisedirect.co.uk

www.franchisesales.co.uk

www.franchiseandbusinessopportunities.co.uk

www.franchiseinfo.co.uk

www.daltonsbusiness.com/franchises-for-sale

www.franchises.co.uk/uk-franchise-opportunities

www.thefranchise-shop.com

www.openfranchise.co.uk

www.selectyourfranchise.com

There are many more but the above should give you a good cross section of business for sale and their costs. As we have stressed, always check their credentials, such as are they a member of the bfa?

There are other recruitment methods in addition to the web. These include adverts in local and national newspapers and magazines. Perhaps the best known trade magazine for business for sale generally, including franchises, is Dalton's Weekly. There are others such as the Daily Express, Franchise World (www.franchiseworld.co.uk) Business Franchise Magazine (www.franchiseinfo.co.uk) The Franchise Magazine (www.thefranchisemagazine.net) and What Franchise Magazine. This last one is the official organ of the bfa (www.bfa.org/members/what-franchise-magazine).

Another way to gain invaluable information, go to seminars and listen to the experiences of other people is to attend an exhibition. The largest of these is the National Franchise Exhibition, held several times a year, usually at large arenas such as the National Exhibition Centre in Birmingham or in Manchester or London. Although these large exhibitions can be a little overwhelming, if you know what you want to get out of them they will prove very educational indeed.

One thing you will get is a birds eye view of many franchises available, of all sizes and their costs available, under one roof. Well worth a visit!

For more information go to www.franchiseinfo.co.uk which will list all of the exhibitions and their sites available during a particular year.

The main exhibition promoters are the National Franchise Exhibition, The British and International Franchise Exhibition and Growing Your Own Business. They usually exhibit at the NEC Birmingham, Olympia London and Event City Manchester, although these venues will vary depending on availability.

Questions to ask franchisors

When you attend exhibitions, you will no doubt meet different franchisors and you will need to ask some very pertinent questions in order to gain a picture of what it is they are offering.

Below are questions you should be asking franchisors generally, not just at exhibitions. Make sure that you write them down so you don't forget them:

- Can you tell me more about your business, an overview of its operations and its vision for the future?
- What support and training do you offer at the outset and also on an ongoing basis?
- Is your business doing well, do you have any past performance figures?
- What is the overall failure rate?
- What are the costs involved in setting up a business with you, both immediate costs and future costs?
- What obstacles do you see to growth in the future years?
- What is the franchise package comprised of and how are the costs apportioned?

You will no doubt have many other questions, but these are the most important. You need to gain a clear view of what it is you are getting involved in, whether you as a person will be suited to what is on offer and whether you can raise the finance.

In the next chapter, we will look at how you go about raising finance to fund the purchase of a franchise and what questions the banks will have, plus also look at the business plan that you will be expected to formulate to back up your requests for finance.

Now read a summary of the main points from Chapter 4 overleaf.

****

Main points from Chapter 4
Searching For the Right Franchise and Asking The Right Questions

- If you want to start a franchise, or are thinking of doing so, the first thing to do is to contact the franchisor direct. There are a number of ways to do this, the most convenient being the internet. As mentioned in the previous chapters, there are numerous sites with details of those companies that offer franchises. Many of the best known brands don't need to advertise that heavily as they will receive many enquiries directly from the public. They then filter out the interested parties and decide who might be suitable for their franchise opportunities.
- When talking to a potential franchisor ask if they are a member of the British Franchise Association and if not, why not?

Chapter 5

Financing a Purchase-Preparing a Business plan

Raising finance for a franchise

For many, one of the biggest hurdles to getting a franchise off the ground is approaching the bank for finance. Before you even think about finance you will need to research your chosen franchise, making sure that it is the right one for you and that you are fully aware of what is involved.

The very first step is to establish how much money you can invest in the business i.e.- what can you afford to invest? Before you go to a bank, are there any other sources of finance for a franchise available, such as from family or friends?

Approaching banks for finance

Banks usually feel that it is safer to lend to franchisees of well-structured ethical franchise systems. The track record of the franchisor is important to a bank when assessing whether to lend finance. With an established franchise, the major banks can lend up to 70% of the start up costs, for new franchises the figure will probably be around 50%. The following are the main points to take into account when considering approaching a bank:

- How much finance will you be able to borrow? You should prepare a full list of your personal expenditure such as mortgage, hire purchase, household bills, and so on. This will show how much money you will need to take out of the business in order to live.

- What security can you give to back up your loan? You might have a life policy with some value, or have equity in your home. Many people use their home as collateral or re-mortgage to finance a business.

Start preparing your business plan - this is a vital document to obtain finance from the bank. Your chosen franchisor will often help you with this. See further on in this chapter for advice on business plans and preparing a cash flow forecast.

Banks generally use the following approach to assess requests for finance.

The person - Who are they lending the money to?
The bank will carry out a full review of your background and reliability, your training, qualifications, and track record, financial resources, suitability to run the business.

A franchisor will also look at this to ensure that you are a suitable franchisee.

The amount - How much are you looking to borrow?
Banks will normally expect the franchisee to contribute at least 30% of the total cost of the franchise, or 50% for a new franchise; this contribution should come from your own resources.

Apart from the actual amount the bank will also look at the purpose for which the money is going to be used and it's effect on your business. They will also look at:

- Is there sufficient demand for your product or service?
- How will the money borrowed benefit the business?
- What is the type of finance you are looking for, is it an overdraft, loan or a package of financial services?

- How much are you yourself investing in the business? Normally you are expected to contribute towards the total start up costs from your own resources

Your franchisor, if it is reputable, will normally help with setting out details of start up funds required and help with the preparation of cash flow forecasts.

How do you intend to pay back the money?
Banks will consider the following:
- Where is repayment coming from?
- What are the future trading profits after allowing for all your other financial commitments?
- What assumptions have been made in the cash flow forecast?
- What levels of sales are needed to break-even and are they achievable?
- Do you have a contingency plan for any setbacks?

How much risk is involved?
The bank will assess the risk of lending to you and decide whether security is required. This will depend on their evaluation of your business as a whole. If no security is available, they may be able to consider finance under the Government's Enterprise Finance Guarantee, if your business is eligible. This is a Government backed scheme to guarantee 75% of borrowing (for businesses both under and over 2 years established) where security is not available and where that lack of security is the only bar to a bank lending the money.

The calculation of interest and fees
When the banks set an interest rate they take into account a number of factors including your stake in the business,

security deposited and their evaluation of the risk involved. There are some special finance schemes for some of the larger, well-established franchisors. They may also charge a fee to cover the costs of setting up new borrowing and completing the security arrangements.

Forms of finance

There are several sources of finance for a franchise available in different formats. Loan accounts are most often used for the purchase of assets e.g. property where the loan will run for a longer period or a vehicle purchase where the term of the loan will be much shorter to reflect the rapid depreciation of the asset. Fixed interest rates are often available.

An alternative method of funding working capital is invoice finance, which involves raising finance using your debtor book. The advantage of this is that cash flow is directly linked to business expansion. This method is not suitable for all businesses and your bank will be able to advise you.

Another method of finance to consider is asset finance to fund the purchase of equipment for the business. This can help ease cash flow by spreading repayments over a period of time instead of making a one-off investment.

Total cost of opening a franchise

It is important that you do your planning and forecasting thoroughly as start-up costs for opening a franchise can vary dramatically based upon the type of franchise involved. Below are the main costs to consider when doing your calculations:

Initial franchise fee
Equipment such as a van or vehicle lease
Funding opening stock
Leasing premises

Refurbishment requirements
Branding, fixtures and fittings
Professional charges such as lawyer, architects and surveyor's fees
Insurance
Recruitment costs
Marketing costs
Working capital
Training costs
Ongoing management services fees

Franchise deposits

Some franchisors may ask prospective franchisees to pay a deposit at a very early stage in the recruitment process - clearly it is vital that you know the terms under which the deposit is taken and what rights it will provide.

There should be a deposit agreement, setting out what territory is being secured and how long for, as well as how and when any deposit would be refunded. Under British Franchise Association rules, the deposit, less any direct expenses actually incurred by the franchisor, should be refundable if the prospective franchisee decides not to go ahead. Deposits are particularly common:

- If the newcomer is buying a franchise business from an existing franchisee of the network, when typically the buyer will pay a 10% deposit on exchange of the sale and purchase agreement;
- If the new franchisee is setting up in a virgin territory and needs to find suitable premises, when the franchisor may ask for a deposit to be paid upfront while the franchisee looks for suitable premises. Once premises are found, the franchisee will sign the

franchise agreement and pay the balance of the franchise fee.

From a franchisee's perspective, paying a deposit may secure their chosen territory and give them exclusivity whilst they carry out further steps in preparation for signing the franchise agreement.

Before you part with any cash, you should ensure that you fully understand why you are being asked to pay a deposit and in what circumstances it will be refunded. The deposit paid should normally be credited against the franchise fee once you have decided to proceed. All legal contracts should be vetted by a solicitor specialising in franchising, including deposit agreements and any confidentiality agreement you may be asked to sign before detailed financial information is made available.

Franchise Fees-Initial franchise fees
The initial franchise fee varies from company to company and is paid by the franchisee when the franchise is granted. The initial franchise fee covers the cost of training, recruiting, territory analysis, site identification, specialist equipment, stationary, franchisee launch, etc. In addition, there will be an element of recovery of franchise development costs by the franchisor.

On-going franchise fees
The on-going franchise fee is usually based upon a percentage of the 'gross revenue' or sales of the franchisee after deducting VAT. There is no set formula; rather it depends on the split of responsibilities between franchisee/franchisor. The more the franchisor does the higher the fee. In some cases there will be no on-going fee - it will be covered in a

mark-up on the product. There are also cases where the franchisor will justify an increase in fees on issues such as extra start-up costs and inflation. In any case the type of fees to be paid, its regularity and whether it can be increased or decreased should correctly reflect the services the franchisor will provide, and should be properly communicated to the franchisee before the franchise agreement is signed. You therefore need to know:

How much the royalty fee is?
How often it is to be paid?
Is it a percentage or fixed amount?
If a percentage, what is it based on?
How does it compare to other franchise systems?

Advertising Fee

Advertising fees are used to advertise the franchise system. Normally an advertising fee is based upon a percentage of gross sales or net sales (though it can sometimes be a stated amount). They typically range from 1% to 5% of gross sales.

The fees are often put into a regional or national fund to be used for either regional or national marketing or advertising campaigns. Franchisors in the start-up phase may not ask for an advertising fee to be paid, as they would not expect to achieve any real benefit, i.e. in terms of increase in sales or brand awareness, via a regional or national campaign. They will however expect the franchisee to pay for local advertising to promote their franchise. You need to know:

What the fee is?
Is the same fee paid throughout the network?
How it compares with other systems?
What you get for your money?

If the franchisor can spend the fee on how they see fit?
Will an advertising fee benefit the system?
Or your franchise?

Franchise Business Plan

Your business plan should outline what you want to do, how much money you need to do it with and how you plan to pay the money back. It should also include a Profit Forecast and Cash Flow Model. These are the fundamental prerequisites of any business plan.

However, there is more to the Business Plan than getting funding. It will help you clarify your ideas and objectives. You will have to answer questions on your business objectives, your product or service, pricing methods, your customers and competition. Many franchisors will assist in the preparation of a business plan.

Preparing and presenting your business plan is a real test of your business acumen. Producing the plan tends to bring everything out into the open, focuses your mind on all elements of the business, and helps put your thoughts down in black and white.

Preparing a business plan

Your Business Plan is the 'sales document' for you and your business. It's preparation and presentation should project the image you want for your business. Its content should be clear, concise, to the point and divided into logical sections. As a guideline, your plan should structure broadly as follows:

1. Introduction

- Describe the purpose of your business, briefly outline the concept. Include your overall business objectives.

- Decide on the 'legal status' of your business - sole trader, partnership, limited company or co-operative? All have benefits and shortcomings. Find out which is right for your situation.

2. The Product or Service

- Describe precisely the product or service that your business will offer. Include any relevant history of the product or service and try to avoid any jargon.
- List the distinctive qualities of your product or service and describe your 'Unique Selling Point' (USP) - the key feature which makes your product or service stand out in the market place.
- Describe how your product or service can be developed in line with a changing market.

3. The Personnel

You should include details of anyone who will be involved in making your business a success. These people are a very important asset and this is therefore a key section of your Business Plan. Include in this section:

- A précis of each person, including their personal assessment of their attributes, strengths and weaknesses as well as your own assessment of each person.
- Their relevant experience, commitment and reasons for involvement in your new venture.

You should also include, if possible, a detailed CV for each person in the 'Appendix' at the end of your plan.

4. The Market

This is probably the most important section of the whole Plan - without a clearly defined market your business will not succeed. If you can show that you have carried out thorough research in this section, you will gain credibility for the whole business plan. Your franchisor will also have research in this area. You should:

- Describe the current conditions in the market place for your product or service.
- Detail any relevant facts and figures relating to the market sector(s) that you will be targeting - for example geographical location, size (in terms of people and money), expected growth, and the type(s) of potential customers for your product or service.

Give details of your competitors and explain why your potential customers will choose your product or service rather than the competition. This is the point where research pays off. You should make use of the wealth of business information that is available about markets, competitors and customers.

5. The Marketing Plan

A business must have a clearly defined marketing plan, which will include:

- Your marketing objectives - for example number of sales or market share.
- Where your product or service will be 'positioned' in the market place in terms of price, quality, image etc.
- What your planned marketing communications are - advertising, leaflets and brochures, etc.

- How your product or service will be distributed and /or sold, e.g. through agents, sales teams, etc.
- What customer care policy is planned and how it will work.

Any interest that you have already generated or details of possible orders you have already taken should be included in the appendix.

6. The Operation

Having an efficient operation can be the key to a profitable business. This section should describe how you will supply your product or service. Your Franchisor will have set systems that you will have to adhere to.

- Include your sources of supply, labour and materials.
- Detail the resources required to operate your business, differentiating between what you already have and what you need to acquire.
- Identify any critical procedures or sensitive issues and outline possible alternatives.
- State where you intend to operate from - your current premises and future requirements.
- Outline your current Health and Safety policies - if you don't comply with your statutory obligations, you will need to take action.

7. The Premises

You need to decide on the most appropriate premises for your business needs together with the franchisor. Whether you are working from home or looking for factory premises, you need to consider the following:

- Location
- Future business growth
- Running costs and Uniform Business Rates
- Insurances
- Planning Consent

8. Financial Information

a) Introduction

Start with a summary of the key facts:

- The forecast profit (or loss) for the year.
- Whether financing is required and if so, how much and where the money is to come from.
- The 'break even' sales for the business should be calculated and shown as a percentage of your anticipated sales.
- Details of the money you need to take out of the business to live on - your required income.

A detailed schedule of your required income should be included in the Appendix.

b) Profit & Loss Forecast

Your forecast profit (or loss) should be based on your anticipated sales, minus your direct costs and overheads. The assumptions made in producing your forecast should be listed:

- Include as much detail as possible to justify anticipated sales.
- Any direct costs (materials etc.) should be detailed

Don't forget your overheads - it is just as important to show how they have been calculated.

c) Cash Flow Forecast

Cash will flow in and out of your business - often at different rates and times for example, you may have to pay for materials in advance, yet wait months for payment after you have sold your product or service.

Situations like this can lead to cash flow problems in an apparently profitable business. To anticipate how much cash your business will require, you should convert your profit and loss forecast into a cash flow forecast. List your assumptions:

- When will you get the money from sales.
- When will you have to pay suppliers.
- The timing of specific overheads.
- How much capital equipment that you require for your business. Differentiate between existing equipment and expenditure still to be made - how much and when.

Properly done, this will tell you when your business is likely to be short of cash and it will enable you to plan for this.

Appendix

This is the final section of your Business Plan. It should include the detailed information mentioned earlier - CV's, details of orders etc. You can also include:

- Details of premises
- Insurance details
- Product brochures, photographs and letterhead

Anything else that you believe will enhance your credibility or enhance the credibility of you or your business.

Verifying a franchisor's projections

One of the simplest and most effective ways to verify the projections given by the franchisor is to speak to other franchisees. All franchisors should be willing to provide you with a list of their franchisees, so that you can contact them to find out what their experience has been and if the financial projections produced by the franchisor were accurate and if not, what the difference was.

You should not be afraid to ask the franchisor to clarify how they have arrived at the figures in any draft business plan or prospectus, as part of your research. In addition, you should obtain a copy of the franchisor's filed accounts and possibly also the filed accounts of some of its franchisees. These are documents of public record, which can be readily obtained and will give an accurate picture of financial status of those businesses.

If you are not confident in looking at these figures, your accountant should be able to give you guidance.

Any projections provided by the franchisor will only be a basis for you to build your own business plan and projections - but they will at least give you a starting point. You should use them to check how you feel about the franchise and whether you want to go ahead. How long will it take you to get payback on your initial outlay, how much will you need to borrow to get the business up and running?

In the next chapter we will look at the nature of the legal agreement that you will be required to enter into, the contract with the franchisor. Many lawyers are familiar with these contracts but it is very important that you are also aware and have read and understood the agreement because once signed it will affect your life considerably.

Now read a summary of the main points from chapter 5 overleaf.

....

Main points from Chapter 5
Financing a Purchase-Preparing a Business plan

- For many, one of the biggest hurdles to getting a franchise off the ground is approaching the bank for finance.
- The very first step is to establish how much money you can invest in the business i.e.- what can you afford to invest? Before you go to a bank, are there any other sources of finance for a franchise available, such as from family or friends?
- Start preparing your business plan - this is a vital document to obtain finance from the bank. Your chosen franchisor will often help you with this.
- The bank will carry out a full review of your background and reliability, your training, qualifications, and track record, financial resources, suitability to run the business. A franchisor will also look at this to ensure that you are a suitable franchisee.
- Banks will normally expect the franchisee to contribute at least 30% of the total cost of the franchise, or 50% for a new franchise; this contribution should come from your own resources.
- Some franchisors may ask prospective franchisees to pay a deposit at a very early stage in the recruitment process - clearly it is vital that you know the terms under which the deposit is taken and what rights it will provide.
- There will be an initial franchise fee to pay along with a possible ongoing fee.
- There will be other fees such as advertising fees.
- Your business plan will reflect all associated costs.

Chapter 6

The Legal Agreement

The franchise agreement

In order to become a franchisee you will have to enter into a legal agreement with the franchisor, known as the franchise agreement.

What is the Franchise Agreement?

A franchise agreement represents a contract between you and the franchisor and should achieve three fundamental objectives:

1. Given the absence of specific franchise legislation, it should contractually bind the franchisor and the franchisee and accurately reflect the terms agreed upon.

2. It should seek to protect for the benefit both of the franchisor and the franchisee and the franchisors intellectual property.

3. It should clearly set out the rules to be observed by the parties.

The Terms of the agreement

As there is no specific legislation or regulation for franchising, the franchise agreement becomes all-important in determining the rights and obligations of the franchisor and the franchisee and the relationship between them. If difficulties should arise between the franchisor and the franchisee they will need to turn to the contract to see what, if any, rights and obligations have been provided in the franchise agreement.

What should I look for in a franchise agreement?
A franchisee will look for agreements:

- To train the franchisee and his/her staff
- To supply goods and / or services
- To be responsible for advertising, marketing and promotions
- To assist the franchisee to locate and acquire property and have it fitted out and converted into a franchised outlet. (Similar considerations apply with regard to the acquisition of vehicles, fitting them out, equipping the franchisee etc.)
- To assist the franchisee to set up in business
- To improve, enhance and develop the business system
- To provide certain management and possibly accounting services

Franchisors will be anxious to ensure that the franchise agreement clearly sets out the obligations of the franchisee.

A franchisor will wish to:

- Monitor the performance of the franchisee
- Protect them from unfair competition
- Protect his intellectual property
- Impose obligations and restrictions on the franchisee with regard to the exercise of the rights granted by him to the franchisee

The Intellectual Property

These are in the nature of:

- Trade Name
- Goodwill
- Methods of Production
- Confidential Information and know-how
- Copyright

Trade Marks and Service Marks

Unless the franchise agreement contains sufficient safeguards to protect the franchisors intellectual property rights, the franchisor may find that he/she is unable to prevent infringement of his /her rights by a third party or an ex-franchisee.

Franchisors should be aware that it is not only in the interests of the franchisor that these rights be protected.

Franchisees are equally concerned to ensure that the franchisor had done everything that is reasonably possible for him to protect the intellectual property rights in question. Many franchisees purchase a particular franchise because of the high profile a franchise enjoys in the market place. In many cases, a franchisee has the choice of which franchise to purchase in the same market sector and one of the reasons why a franchisee will have chosen a particular franchise is because of its strong brand image. It follows therefore that the franchisee will be anxious to ensure that in the event of infringement, the franchisor has taken sufficient steps to safeguard his ownership in his intellectual property rights so that he can stop infringement and thereby protect the reputation of that brand name both for himself and for his franchise network.

Brand names and trademarks are becoming increasingly important to business; they can increase the asset value of a company and therefore need to be adequately protected. The franchise agreement should therefore not only grant relevant rights to the franchisee and reserve rights for the franchisor, but should also contain mechanisms necessary for protecting the franchisors intellectual rights from infringement.

The Rules

The franchise agreement should be in a standard form with all prospective franchisees being offered the same terms with no special deals being done. If a franchise agreement is to be non-negotiable then it is important, from the franchisees point of view, that it is well balanced in terms of rights and obligations of the parties and takes into consideration the franchisees concerns also.

If you are serious about buying a franchise, it is imperative that you get your franchise legal advice from an experienced franchise solicitor. *Whichfranchise* and the BFA has a list of accredited franchise legal advisors.

The franchise agreement should clearly:

- Specify in detail the duties and obligations both of the franchisor and of the franchisee
- State the grounds upon which the franchisor will seek to terminate the franchise agreement
- Deal with the payment of franchise fees and the timing of those payments
- Set out the consequences of such termination

Franchisors should be aware that under English law if an ambiguity arises in a franchise agreement the Courts will tend to interpret the ambiguity in favour of the franchisee. They reason that, as the draftsman of the contract, it is the franchisors responsibility to make sure that he/she gets it right and therefore they will not allow him/her to benefit from any ambiguity which may well arise as a result of unclear drafting.

Some thought has to be given to the franchisees and their objectives and provision should therefore be made in the franchise agreement to deal with what is to happen should the franchisee die or become permanently incapacitated .

It is also advisable to deal with the question of what is to happen if a franchisee wishes to sell his business during the term of his franchise agreement . Here, as in other matters, a balance has to be struck between the need of the franchisee to realise his/her investment as and when he/she wants to and the requirement of the franchisor to approve those coming into the franchise network and to prevent those leaving the network (for whatever reason) from continuing to use the franchisors trade secrets and competing unfairly.

The franchise transaction is complex and the franchise agreement must respect that complexity. Experience has shown that those franchisors who take the matter of the franchise contract lightly pay dearly for their mistake.

To the franchisee, the franchise contract represents an investment. His/her business depends upon it to the extent that his business may disappear should it terminate. For the franchisor, the franchise agreement is an income producing asset which will ultimately have a place on his/her balance sheet.

Now read a summary of the main points from chapter 6 overleaf.

....

Main points from Chapter 6
The Legal Agreement

- In order to become a franchisee you will have to enter into a legal agreement with the franchisor, known as the franchise agreement.
- A franchise agreement represents a contract between you and the franchisor and should achieve three fundamental objectives:

1. Given the absence of specific franchise legislation, it should contractually bind the franchisor and the franchisee and accurately reflect the terms agreed upon.
2. It should seek to protect for the benefit both of the franchisor and the franchisee and the franchisors intellectual property.
3. It should clearly set out the rules to be observed by the parties.

- The franchise agreement should be in a standard form with all prospective franchisees being offered the same terms with no special deals being done. If a franchise agreement is to be non-negotiable then it is important, from the franchisees point of view, that it is well balanced in terms of rights and obligations of the parties and takes into consideration the franchisees concerns also.
- If you are serious about buying a franchise, it is imperative that you get your franchise legal advice from an experienced franchise solicitor. Whichfranchise and the BFA has a list of accredited franchise legal advisors.

Chapter 7

The Franchise Operations Manual and Franchise Training

The operations manual outlines everything a franchisee needs to know about running their franchise business and executes the obligations outlined in the franchise agreement. It provides franchise guidelines for running a successful replicate of the franchisors business.

The operations manual provides the franchisee with support and guidance and helps the franchisee to meet the quality of standards expected of them by the franchisor. It also ensures consistency across the network which in turn helps the franchisor to protect their brand. Every franchisee in the network is therefore singing off the same hymn sheet.

In order for the franchisee to follow the manual accurately it needs to be detailed and informative. Each manual will depend on the nature of the business, e.g. franchises that are in the food industry will need to cover health and safety as well as food hygiene in their manual. Overall this franchise guide should generally cover the following:

About the company – its' history, who runs the company, who the legal advisors are, the aims and objectives of the company.

Support – what support the franchisee will receive, who the support team is and how to go about getting the right support i.e. channels of communication.

Launch timetable – what needs to be done and by when, what the obligations of the company are to assist the franchisee in the opening of their new franchise.

Training – what training the franchisee will receive, who takes the training, what training qualifications the company has, what additional training the franchisee should expect to receive after the franchise has been launched, any national sales meetings the company runs.

Recruiting staff – what positions the franchisee needs to fill, what should be in the job description and what skills the applicants should posses.

Office policies – how to set up the office, customer service standards, process for dealing with complaints, employee dress code, managing visitors, computer usage and access policy.

Office maintenance – housekeeping duties, daily procedure for opening and closing the business, the responsibilities of staff, office cleaning, office administration, health and safety and inventory maintenance.

Office equipment – what the franchisee is given, how to maintain it and list of approved suppliers for further purchases.

Administration – record keeping, accounts and finance.

Reporting – the procedures the franchisee should use for reporting back to the franchisor, what happens if the report is not sent over and other records and reports need to be kept for audits and inspections.

Vehicle administration – leasing of cars and the policy for dealing with auto crime.

Marketing – the requirements, who the target audience is, and how best to target this audience using the most effective media channels.

Pricing – how you set prices and fee structures.

Sales – managing leads and referrals, telephone selling procedure and sales presentations.

Insurance – what insurances are required, and what is covered within these policies, the suppliers to use and risk management and security.

Corporate structure – setting up the franchise business, what the different types of structure and legal requirements.

Financing – who the existing financing agreements are with, what alternative financing is available.

Company protection - information on using copyrights, proprietary and trademarks, and how to avoid misuse.

Field operations – looks at health and safety outside of the office and risk management.

Resale, transfer, renewal and closing of the business – conditions for renewal, procedures for business transfer, termination of the business.

Expansion and relocation – what the procedures are if you wish to expand a new or an existing territory and also if you wish to relocate the business.

Franchise support

Having established that the franchise is reputable, and it is a business you see yourself being part of, you then need to examine the strengths and weaknesses of their franchise operation.

You need to be comfortable that they will provide you with the required support you need at the launch of your franchise business and on an ongoing basis. This is central to the success of your franchise.

If you receive no or little support, your business will be on a downward spiral from the start. You will have no one to turn to when problems arise and will continue to make the same errors time after time. You will become demoralized and start to detest going into work each day.

A good franchise company will be available 24/7 to help you with any problems you have. They will be there throughout your launch and will continue to provide you with the dedicated support you need on an ongoing basis. They should provide you with a detailed operations manual that outlines all areas of running your business.

They will have support teams in place to deal with your queries and will regularly visit you at your workplace to make sure that you are coping and to make sure that the business is being run efficiently.

Also ask the franchisor and franchisees about implementing change and what support you would receive e.g. new computer systems, rebranding, new product development etc.

Ask:

- How do they support your marketing activities? Who does what and what is provided?

- Do they offer cover if you go on vacation? What happens if you are ill, what support do they provide?

- What support would you receive to help you with staff recruitment and training? Do they train your staff for you or train you to train your staff? Or do they not offer any training support?

Good franchisors will hold an annual conference where franchisees can get together to discuss any issues or ideas they have, and to hear from the franchisor on their plans to take the business forward.

The franchisor should also assist with making sure that you have the correct insurance for your business as well as any certificates and accreditations you may require e.g. health and safety.

Ask other franchisees what support they receive and what changes they would make. This is the best way to get an insight into the business. You need to be happy with the results of all your research before you should consider entering into an agreement with the franchisor.

Franchise training

It is essential to evaluate what training you should expect to receive from the franchise you are interested in.

A good franchisor will invest heavily in training their franchisees so that they provide them with all the skills they need to make their franchise a success; a bad franchisor is only after your money!

The ethical franchisor will make sure that their franchisees and their staff are fully prepared in all aspects of operating the business before letting them open.

The training is uniform across the network so that all franchisees operate the business in the same way. This consistency helps to ensure long term success for both the franchisee and the franchisor.

The franchisor is responsible for ensuring that they provide training that is competitive and current.

Training can take the format of "classroom training" which usually happens at Head Office in a dedicated training room, and "hands-on" training where you are trained in either an actual franchise unit or an operating unit that has been built in Head Office and which mirrors that of an actual franchise outlet; hands-on allows you to grasp how everything physically works.

Most franchisors will offer a combination of the two. The training will be undertaken by a skilled and qualified instructor who knows how the business operates inside and out and can take up to 8 weeks.

You will also have a training team with you during your first few weeks of trading to make sure that you remember everything the training taught you, and to offer their experience on running the franchise. This on-site training is invaluable.

If the company introduces change, new systems, products etc, the franchisor should make sure that the change does not disrupt the network and that all franchisees are comfortable with the change. To do this they will make sure that adequate training is given.

Your training should also have covered how to recruit and train staff. This is important if your franchise is a retail business where the nature of the work means that staff turnover can be high. You will need to be able to recruit and train staff effectively and efficiently.

The Franchise Agreement should outline the franchisor's obligation to the franchisee i.e. what they are committed to provide. Does it look sufficient? Does it look value for money?

Now read a summary of the main points from chapter 7 overleaf.

....

Main points from Chapter 7
The Franchise Operations Manual and Franchise Training

- The operations manual outlines everything a franchisee needs to know about running their franchise business and executes the obligations outlined in the franchise agreement. It provides franchise guidelines for running a successful replicate of the franchisors business.

- The operations manual provides the franchisee with support and guidance and helps the franchisee to meet the quality of standards expected of them by the franchisor. It also ensures consistency across the network which in turn helps the franchisor to protect their brand. Every franchisee in the network is therefore singing off the same hymn sheet.

- In order for the franchisee to follow the manual accurately it needs to be detailed and informative. Each manual will depend on the nature of the business, e.g. franchises that are in the food industry will need to cover health and safety as well as food hygiene in their manual.

- It is essential to evaluate what training you should expect to receive from the franchise you are interested in.

....

Chapter 8

The Ongoing Management of your Business

The initial phase of the business

After you have completed the purchase of the franchise, signed the contract, obtained the finance and received your initial training, which can take upwards of two months or more, the main task is now getting your business up and running. Depending on the type of franchise you have bought, you will probably be heavily reliant on the support of your franchisor.

The initial training can vary depending on the franchisor and can involve spending time at other franchise premises, receiving training over the phone and face to face training. All in all, don't miss training sessions as they will be vital.

In the first instance, depending on the type of franchise, there will be certain areas of your operation to attend to, such as finding premises (some franchisors will do this for you), hire staff and develop relationships with suppliers.

Finding premises

This is obviously very important and is an area where you will need advice. The premises that you choose very much depends on what is that you are selling-location is all important. You will need to look carefully and most franchisors will help, some will even go as far as doing all the work for you-such as Subway sandwiches. However, you will need time here as like any business there is the time period between signing your agreement and actually finding and equipping the premises, which can take anything up to a year, depending on the complexity of the business.

Buying equipment

Another area to attend to is investing in certain types of equipment. Again, what you buy will depend totally on what the franchise is. As it is a franchise you will no doubt be required to buy certain types of equipment that are uniform to all of the franchises. Many franchisors will operate a turnkey scheme, which means that all the equipment needed to run a franchise will be supplied to you and will be included in the overall price. This certainly makes life easier. Even if your franchise package does not include equipment you should be advised by your franchisor on what is needed and where you can source it and what the cost is and also the best options, such as leasing as opposed to buying. With leasing, you can employ your capital elsewhere rather than tying it up, which will be very important in the early days.

Recruiting staff

This is an area where you will certainly need help. Having said this, if you have considerable experience in the industry that you have chosen then you will know where to look. The following are things that you need to know.

Employing People

At first you may be able to run your business by yourself or with help from your family. But if not, or as your business expands, you may need to employ people. Before doing this, some businesses may consider it worthwhile subcontracting work. This may be more cost effective in ironing out short-term trading highs and lows. However, if you do need to take on employees, then you must do certain things.

What are my responsibilities as an employer?

You must give every employee a written statement of terms of employment. At the time of publication, by law, all employees working 16 or more hours a week must be given a written statement of terms after they have worked 13 weeks in the job. This statement must include the following:

- name of employer
- name of employee, job title and description
- hours of work
- pay details, including how often the employee is paid
- holidays
- grievance procedures
- sickness and injury procedures
- pension schemes
- length of notice needed to end employment
- disciplinary rules, including dress and behaviour

Discrimination and the law

It is against the law for an employer or a would-be employer to advertise a job that any way discriminates against race or sex. After taking on an employee, the anti-discrimination laws still apply to all other parts of the employees job, including wages and holidays.

Again, the advice that you receive in this area will very much depend on the franchisor. Many will run training programmes as, in addition to knowing the basics you will need to know how to interview staff, where to advertise etc. You will also need to know how to operate payroll systems and know about wages and national insurance, pension responsibilities etc.

If the above sounds daunting, you can take comfort in the fact that the bigger franchisors will often send a team of experienced franchisees to help and assist during the early period when you are finding your feet. Therefore, you won't have the feeling that you are alone!

Now read a summary of the main points from chapter 8 overleaf.

....

Main points from Chapter 8

- After you have completed the purchase of the franchise, signed the contract, obtained the finance and received your initial training, which can take upwards of two months or more, the main task is now getting your business up and running.
- In the first instance, depending on the type of franchise, there will be certain areas of your operation to attend to, such as finding premises (some franchisors will do this for you), hire staff and develop relationships with suppliers.

....

Part 2

Basic Tips on Running a Business

FINANCIAL CONTROL, PRODUCTS AND MARKETS AND MARKETING GENERALLY

Chapter 9

Basic Tips on Running a Business-Financial Control

Although you will get support and training from your franchisor, at least with many of the businesses on offer, there are key fundamental skills and areas of knowledge that you will need to be conversant with in the control and development of business: financial control and record keeping; pricing your products (although this again will vary with different franchises, as some will have national prices); marketing and customer service. Even if you are to receive a grounding in these areas it is always worthwhile going over them to raise awareness of the business environment. The larger franchises will take care of these areas for you but many of the smaller franchises won't and you will need to employ this knowledge yourself to grow your business. We will first deal with financial control

Financial Control

Here, we will consider the importance of financial control within the process of business planning. In particular, we will look at profit and loss forecasting, cashflow forecasting, effective bookkeeping, and tax and insurance.

Profit and loss forecasting

A profit and loss forecast is a projection of what sales you think you will achieve, what costs you will incur in achieving those sales and what profit you will earn. Having this information down on paper means that you will be able to refer to it, and adjust it as your business develops.

Cashflow forecast

A cashflow forecast, as the name suggests, forecasts the changes in the cash which comes into and out of your bank account each month. For example, your customers may pay you after one month, whereas you might pay out for rent or insurance in advance. At the same time, you will have to pay for certain costs such as materials or wages and will need to budget for this.

Preparing a Cashflow Forecast

Remember that a cashflow forecast helps you to evaluate the timing of money coming into and going out of your business. In showing you the "movement" of money it takes full account of the fact that you may often not be paid immediately for work done and, correspondingly, that you may not have to pay immediately for goods and services you acquire. An important purpose of a cashflow forecast is to reveal the gap between your cash receipts and payments. It will show you whether or not, for example, you might need to borrow, and if so, when you are most likely to require additional funds. It is very common for businesses to need more cash as they grow because of the difference in timing of receipts and payments.

Other Terms

Working Capital-Working capital is the term often used to describe the short-term resources used by the business for everyday trading purposes. This consists of:

Debtors-these are customers you have sold to in credit, i.e., they owe you money.

Creditors-these are your suppliers who you have purchased from on credit, i.e. you owe them money.

Stock-this represents the value of materials you have purchased. They may be purchased for immediate resale or they may be in the process of being converted into a finished article.

Cash-this can either be the amount of physical cash you are holding or it may be money held in a current or bank deposit account. All of the above have to be carefully controlled if your business is to prosper.

Over-trading

A problem common to many small and growing businesses is what is described as "over trading". The more sales you make, the more money you will need to spend on funding material and debtors before you are paid for the sales. If your level of sales becomes too high and you do not have the necessary level of working capital to support it, you may simply run out of cash. This can be disastrous for your business and means that a full order book is not the only thing to strive for. Even with a profitable business and a full order book, it is imperative to have enough cash available. Extra finance can help your cashflow and make it easier to avoid the pitfalls of over trading.

Check your customer's ability to pay

Before you offer customers credit, check that they can meet their liabilities. You may want to take up bank references.

Set out your terms of trading

Be specific about when you expect payment, for example, 30 days from the date of the invoice and make your customer aware in advance of work that you do.

Set up a system

Set up a system which enables you to issue invoices promptly and shows you when invoices become overdue.

Keep clear and accurate records

Inaccurate invoices or unclear records can be one of the main reasons for customers delaying payments. Make sure you send invoices punctually, to the right person at the right address.

Collect your payment on time

Establish a collections routine and stick to it. Keep records of all correspondence and conversations. Give priority to your larger accounts, but chase smaller amounts too. If regular chasing does not produce results consider stopping further supplies to the customer. If payment is not obtained, don't hesitate to ask a reputable debt collection agency or solicitor to collect the money for you. Your Business activities will consist of selling goods and/or services. At the same time you will have to spend money on behalf of the business, on the purchase or rent of premises, raw materials, equipment, stationery etc. etc. in order to conduct business.

Remember that every business transaction generates a financial transaction, all of which must be recorded in books of account on an on-going basis. It is a fundamental management requirement that this be done on a regular basis, at a minimum once a week. Leave it much longer, and sooner or later an iron law of accounting will come into operation. You will have mislaid a financial record or simply forgotten to request one or issue one. When you do get round to up-dating the books, they won't balance. Unless you can discover the error before the end of the financial year your accountant will be faced with the task of reconciling "incomplete records", which he or she will enjoy because of the professional challenge but which costs you more money for more of his/her time.

What information must be kept?

As a minimum you must keep records of the following: -

i) All the invoices raised (or rendered) on behalf of the business, either when the goods are delivered or the services supplied, or shortly afterwards. An invoice is a legal document and constitutes a formal demand for money. It must provide enough information to identify the business which sent it, who it was sent to, what it is for and whether VAT is payable.

ii) A list of your Sales invoices numbered sequentially.

iii) All Purchase invoices received, and listed i.e. those demands made on your business for the payment of money.

iv) Wages and salaries paid, and to whom; Income tax and NI contributions paid over to the Tax authorities.

v) All chequebook stubs, paying-in slips/books, counterfoils of petty cash vouchers, business bank account statements. Without these you cannot compile your books of account.

vi) A full record of VAT, whether paid by or paid to the business.

The advantages of a bookkeeping system for your business

a) To provide accurate information sufficient to assess whether you are managing the business at a profit or a loss, or whether the business is solvent i.e. is there enough cash available in the business to pay all the outstanding liabilities on demand? The right information of the right kind at the right time is a vital management tool. Good management means making informed decisions of the right kind at the right time based on information that is true and therefore trustworthy.

b) To provide the information required for correct assessments of VAT and Income Tax, so as to avoid financial penalties (and possibly a suspect reputation) for incorrect and/or late payments. HMRC keep records for seven years, and so must you. Your accountant will need the best information in order to minimise your tax liabilities, unless of course you decide to submit a statement of income to your Inspector of Taxes without recourse to an accountant. In any event the Inspector will require a calculation of your Income from the business in the form of an Income and Expenditure Account for each trading year.

c) To monitor the behaviour of the business over time by reference to financial summaries "at a glance". You don't need to remember for example how many meals were served in your restaurant business say in this year compared with last year. The comparison that matters is the financial one with reference to the value of those transactions.

How to record the information you need

There are basically four methods of bookkeeping. Which one to choose will depend largely on the type and size of business you have established. Take advice from a business adviser or accountant if you are unsure as to which is the best one for your needs.

a) Proprietary systems.

These are best suited for sole traders in cash transaction types of business e.g. jobbing builders, market traders or some small shopkeepers. This type of business requires daily record keeping, often including till- rolls for the cash till and offers a simple method of control over finances.

A number of pre-printed stationery systems are available at business bookshops. Select one that allows you enough space to record all that needs recording. Worked examples are set out at the beginning of each book to show you how to keep cash records and the bank position, which can be calculated by following the instructions included. A list of business stationary systems publishers is found at the end of the book.

Cash businesses are more vulnerable than other types for the following reasons: -

i) It is far easier to lose or misplace paperwork. Therefore it is easier to lose control and lose money. Therefore it is more difficult to plan for the future.
ii) It is far more difficult to separate the cash that belongs in the business from the cash belonging to the proprietor.
iii) HMRC pay far closer attention to cash businesses because of the greater scope for "creative accounting" and tax evasion.

To minimise these risks, cash business-proprietors are strongly advised to pay their daily cash takings into the bank by using pre-printed paying-in books supplied by their bank. It is also vital to obtain receipts for purchases made from the takings and to keep them in an orderly fashion.

b) The Analysed Cash book System.
This is perhaps the most common method used by small businesses selling mostly on credit, with perhaps some cash sales. It relies on the Single Entry system of bookkeeping, where each entry is, as the name implies, made once only, and all entries are made in one book, the cashbook.

The analysed cashbook is the "bible" of the business. It allows "at a glance" analysis because it is arranged on a columnar basis, showing how much has been received into the business, when and from where, how much of each receipt is attributable to VAT and therefore how much is the net amount belonging to the business. All this information is written up on one side of a pre-printed book, the left-hand page, showing all monies paid into the bank on behalf of the business. On the opposite, right-hand page are set out in separate columns details of what has been spent by the business, in other words, monies paid out of the bank, to whom and when.

c) The Double Entry System

This method of recording accounts relies on ledgers, or separate books of account for each type of transaction. Far greater detail and control are possible using this system. As well as a cash account there is scope for setting up other ledgers such as the bought ledger for purchases, sales ledger, nominal (or business expense) ledger, salaries and so on. It is much easier to monitor how much has been spent over a period of time on each type of transaction, simply by referring to the particular ledger or account, on each of which a running balance is struck. Every transaction is recorded in the major account called the Cash Account and also in the appropriate subsidiary ledger. In this way the Cash Account acts as a "Control" account for all the separate accounts of the business.

The most important feature of this system is the characterisation of all bookkeeping entries as either a "credit" ("he trusts" i.e." the business owes him") or "debit" ("he owes"). The sophistication of this method lies in the use of two entries for each transaction. For each credit entry in the Cash Account there must be a corresponding debit entry for the same amount in a different account. Likewise for each debit entry in the Cash

Account there must be a corresponding credit entry in a different account. The key words are "equal and opposite". That way the greatest possible degree of control is obtained.

d) Computerised Accounting Systems

A wide variety of off-the-shelf packages are available, which rely on single or double entry methods. It may be tempting to invest in an accounts package at the outset, especially if you intend to use other computer packages in the business. It would be most unwise to start using such a package without understanding the principles that underlie them. Businesses have failed because of the familiar - "GIGO" - garbage in, garbage out. Money is the lifeblood of the business so don't turn it into garbage by neglecting an understanding of the what, why and how of bookkeeping.

Now read the main points overleaf from Chapter 9.

....

Main points from Chapter 9

Financial Control

- Although you will get support and training from your franchisor, with many of the businesses on offer, there are key fundamental skills and areas of knowledge that you will need to be conversant with in the control and development of business: financial control and record keeping; pricing your products (although this again will vary with different franchises, as some will have national prices); marketing and customer service.

....

Chapter 10

Products, Markets and Pricing

The area of markets and pricing is, without doubt, one of the most important areas of a business and the one which is usually neglected. Research and analysis of your potential market, whatever you are making or offering, and however you are choosing to sell it, online or offline, is absolutely crucial to the success of your business.

Without customers to buy your products you cannot survive. With any marketing strategy, there are a number of questions that need to be answered at the outset:

- Who are the potential customers?
- What do they buy and why do they buy it?
- When do they buy and where do they buy?

The above questions are not exhaustive but are the key questions when carrying out initial research. Also important is the nature of the customer, how old, occupation, standard of education and income and family position, i.e. married, single, children and also their location. All these are important factors and research should help to shape your business plan. Although this type of market research might seem too heavy initially, it will prove invaluable as your business develops.

Segmenting the market place
There are a number of different ways to segment customers and markets. There is no one perfect method.

Geographic segmentation

This is a simple form of segmentation and is relatively unsophisticated, consisting of dividing your market on the basis of geographical location of potential customers This is fine if all sales are made within one particular market. For example, if you are selling in the UK then you can segment customers by region.

Demographic segmentation

Demographic segmentation is a more sophisticated way of segmenting customers as it involves identifying potential customers according to specific variables such as age, sex, family size, income or lifestyle. There are two main methods used to provide the different socio-economic groupings, the first classifies occupation and social class groups the second, known as ACORN (A Classification of residential Neighbourhoods) classifies types of neighbourhoods.

Occupation and social class

Here groups are segmented into 6 classes, A to E. Each one denotes a social class type as follows:

A = Higher managerial
B = Intermediate management
C1= Supervisor/ lower management
C2= Skilled manual
D = Semi-skilled/unskilled
E = Lowest level of subsistence

However, when making assumptions about social class, care and skill is required as many assumptions such as disposable income may not be accurate.

ACORN

This method analyses people, or households, on the basis of the type of property. The information is derived from the census, undertaken every ten years with the last one undertaken in 2011. This system is based on the assumption that consumer lifestyles and behaviour are closely related to neighbourhood types.

Again, an alphabetical system is used, A to K, as follows:

A = Modern family housing for manual workers
B = Modern family housing for higher incomes
C = Older housing of intermediate status
D = Poor quality older terraced housing
E = Rural areas
F = Urban local authority housing
G = Housing with most overcrowding
H = Low income areas with migrants
I = Students and high status non-family areas
J = Transitional high status suburbia
K = Areas of elderly people

Product segmentation

This is a simple form of segmentation which is used to identify people who would buy, or potentially buy, a particular product.

Benefit and lifestyle segmentation

This takes demographic segmentation one step further by linking the lifestyle of consumers to their decision to buy a particular product. The next step is to differentiate their product, either on quality or other claimed advantages. As we all know, quite often one product is the same as another. However, the manufacturer will differentiate his or her product by branding and association. Different groups will respond to different messages, such as the ability of toothpaste to prevent tooth decay and to whiten the teeth and so on.

Competitive advantage

This is critical to all marketing. Businesses must differentiate their products from each other in order to gain market share. Competitive advantage can consist of either lower product prices or a better service than competitors. It is crucial that you understand your competitors if you are to obtain a competitive advantage. It is very important that you have as much information about your competitors as possible. You need to:

- Establish exactly who your competitors are
- Identify their marketing objectives
- Analyse their marketing strategies.

You should also look at whether they have any strengths and weaknesses. You can analyse their strengths and weaknesses, and also your own, by carrying out a SWOT analysis. SWOT is the acronym for Strengths, Weaknesses, Opportunities and Threats. A SWOT analysis is compiled using a grid to enable you to consider how you will match your strengths to your opportunities and how you can overcome your weaknesses and threats. Strengths and opportunities are listed in the left hand column and weaknesses and threats are listed in the right column.

See overleaf.

Strengths	Weaknesses
Something that you are doing well or are good at. It could be a skill, competence or competitive advantage that you have over your business rivals.	Something that, by comparison to your rivals, you do poorly. This is a position that puts you at a disadvantage.
Opportunities	Threats
Look for realistic growth opportunities in the business	This is a factor that could lead to problems within your business and subsequent decline.

Unique selling points (USP)

This is a crucial element in defining the competitive advantage of your business. Identifying your Unique Selling Points will help you define what it is that makes you different from your competitors. You can use USP's in your marketing. There are a number of questions that need to be asked when identifying USP's:

- Will the customer perceive this as an advantage?
- Is it very different from what my competitors are offering?
- Will customers receive some benefit from the USP?
- Will the USP motivate customers to make a purchase?

Obviously, an advantage (or perceived advantage) must offer and give benefits over and above your competitor's products.

Within all markets there are a number of factors that will be critical to your success. Examples of critical success factors will be delivery time, speed of service, quality of the product and competitive pricing. Critical success factors will vary from industry to industry and market to market. There is no clear formula as to what will be important and crucial to you. It is vital that you identify your own critical success factors.

Pricing Your Product

A well thought out pricing plan is essential to the future prosperity of your business, and will also help you to make the most of your opportunities.

To develop the right pricing plan for your business, you need to start by working out what your costs are. You need to look at what your competitors are charging and try to estimate what your service or product is worth to your customers.

By knowing what costs you are incurring, you will be able to work out what your "break even" point is. How much do you need to sell before your business covers all its costs, including your own (essential) drawings, but before it makes a profit. Unless you can identify what your break-even point is, you could operate at a loss, without realising until it is too late.

Your Costs

Costs can be divided into fixed (overheads) and variable (direct) costs. Fixed costs include your essential personal expenses, such as mortgage, food etc, as well as rent, heating and lighting wages and interest charges. They tend to stay the same no matter how much you sell. Variable costs, however, increase or decrease according to your level of sales.

The most obvious cost here is the actual cost of materials required to manufacture the product but can include other things such as transport, postage or additional labour. The price you charge for your product has to cover all of the variable costs and contribute towards your overheads.

Outlined below is an example of a break-even point.

Fred Peters Car Wash Ltd	Cost per Annum £
Personal Drawings	10,000
National Insurance	294
Tax	500
Stationary	100
Advertising	400
Telephone	320
Depreciation of Van (over 5 years)	1,000
Petrol	900
Servicing	300
Road Tax Fund	130
Insurance	320
Business Insurance	140
Materials	200
Depreciation of Equipment	200
Bank Loan £3,000 @ 12%	200

Bank Charges	100
Accountants Fees	300
TOTAL	£15,404

Fred's essential personal drawings to cover his family expenses is £10,000. He operates a small car wash. He expects to work for 46 weeks a year, allowing for holidays, sickness etc. He estimates that he will work 38 hours per week.

His annual output is therefore:

46 weeks a year Times 38 hours times 0.5 cars per hour = 874

His break even point is

15,404

―――――

874

= £17.62 per car

After researching the market in his area, Fred believes he can confidently charge £20 per car, which will give him a reasonable profit.

Competitors Prices

Unless your service or product is much better than others on the market, you would be unwise to charge a price which is too far above your competitors, as you will find sales very hard to achieve. On the other hand, a low price often implies low quality or low standards. Competing on price alone is a poor option. It is especially important for small businesses to differentiate themselves by other means, such as personal service, convenience or special skills. Customers rarely buy on price alone and it is worth remembering that you can more easily reduce your prices than put them up.

If, when you work out what your prices should be, they do not cover your costs-look again at how you might make your business viable. For example, could you reduce any of your variable costs, could you get supplies more cheaply, can you negotiate a discount or find an alternative supplier? On your fixed costs, could you trim any other expenditure?

Think again about what you are offering. Could it be improved and sold at a higher price? Can you sell different products for more money to increase your profits? Would sales increase if you put up your prices and spent the extra income on advertising and promotion?

Every cost incurred in running your business must be recovered either by what you charge for your time, or by the amount you charge for your products. Profits will be made only after all of your costs have been covered. But you may decide to use different prices in different situations. For example, a plumber offering a 24 hour service might decide to charge a premium rate for his services if he is called out during the night to deal with an emergency, a different rate for weekends and another rate for normal working hours.

Achieving a range of prices for the variety of skills offered, taking into account the time you would be likely to spend on each job and the convenience factor your customers can give you the flexibility to stay competitive, yet still provide a satisfactory income.

Now read a summary of the main points from Chapter 10 overleaf.

Main points from Chapter 10
Products, Markets and Pricing

- The area of markets and pricing is, without doubt, one of the most important areas of a business and the one which is usually neglected. Research and analysis of your potential market, whatever you are making or offering, and however you are choosing to sell it, online or offline, is absolutely crucial to the success of your business.

- There are a number of different ways to segment customers and markets. There is no one perfect method.

- Identifying your Unique Selling Points will help you define what it is that makes you different from your competitors.

- A well thought out pricing plan is essential to the future prosperity of your business, and will also help you to make the most of your opportunities.

****

Chapter 11

Marketing

The next step in developing your business is to look at sales, and how you are going to achieve them which in turn means looking at the market and considering the most appropriate form of market research. Sales are vital to any business. Whatever you produce, you must be able to sell. This is necessary in order to survive. This chapter covers traditional forms of marketing and also techniques used in online marketing.

You must be satisfied that there is a demand for your proposed products and you must be able to determine how you can investigate the market in which you want to operate, how many potential clients there are in either the catchment area you operate in or the wider area. If you work in publishing for example then clearly the market for your product would be different for that of a baker or butcher or plumber. A lot of thought needs to be given to this area.

Market Research

The tool that is used to determine demand for a product is market research. Market research can be cheap and simple or highly complex depending on how you approach it and what you might want to find out.

Market research, or effective market research should be able to provide you with information as to what people want and also how much they want and what they will pay for it. Competition which might exist should also come to light.

You should not be put off by competition nor should you believe that because there appears to be no local supplier that what you produce will sell. No supplier may mean no demand and competition may mean established demand.

The concept behind all market research is simple-the practice is often not and unless you have a lot of money the costs may be prohibitive. A good example might be a supermarket.

A potential supermarket would want to know concrete facts in order to establish demand. For example, in terms of the percentage of the population, the average number of visits made to a supermarket each year. This they may well be able to establish from their own records if they are part of a chain.

Secondly they would want to know, what distance people are prepared to travel in order to visit a supermarket. This will vary a lot but they would be interested in establishing a national average.

With these two facts the supermarket can then establish the catchment area population for the proposed supermarket. Now they need to know something about the competition. How many supermarkets are there in the catchment zone which might have an effect on the proposed supermarket? This is easily established. However, more difficult to determine is the effect on your potential business. If we suppose that the supermarket decides that only 30% of the catchment area is exposed to competition and that they expect that 50% of that 30% would continue to use the supermarkets they presently use. This means an adjustment to predicted customer base.

However, competition comes from other shops not just supermarkets. This is why calculations are based on average figures since this additional competition will be fairly standard throughout the country. A survey will be carried out in the locality to check that there are no special factors to consider-special factors which may cause adjustments to the predicted customer base either way.

The next question to be considered is; what is the average spend per visit per customer? Supermarkets will almost certainly be able to answer that one from existing records.

From this data, they can predict gross sales and so the net operating profit. If this is not high enough to justify the expenditure, they might be reluctant to proceed with siting a supermarket.

The above is a simple model and does not take into account a number of complications but it does give an idea of how market research is carried out. There are two very important factors to be considered-average conditions in the industry and catchment area population, or a knowledge of that population. Although the example given covers selling to the general public the same principle applies when considering selling to other business.

It may be possible to determine industry averages by approaching trade associations. A visit to the bank is also very worthwhile as most high street banks keep statistics which they would be willing to make available. A further source of statistics might be a major supplier in an industry.

Somewhat easier is to determine the magnitude of the target market. Businesses generally fall into one or two categories: those where the customer comes to the business to place the order and those where the business goes to the customer to get the order.

In the first category, the size of your target market will be a percentage of the local population. The size of the population can be found by contacting the records office at your local authority. The percentage which applies to your proposed business will be far harder to determine. The classic method is simple-ask a large enough sample to provide an accurate picture. This is easier said than done. A great deal of research experience is necessary in order to be able to design a questionnaire which can elicit all the right information.

If you can afford it, you could consider employing a market research agency to assist you. If you cannot afford it then you should spend time considering exactly what you want to ask and what you are trying to establish. There are many other places which will hold the sort of information you might need. Your local training enterprise agency (TEC) or the trade association relevant to your business will be only too pleased to assist you.

Once you have established your target market, you might wish to consider exactly how you sell to that market. Easy if you have a shop in the middle of a busy shopping area, at least easier than if you produce books and have to cast your net far wider. It might be useful at this stage to look at marketing in a little more depth.

Bringing people's attention to your product

Although the relationship with your franchisor and the marketing that they offer will affect how much marketing you do, it is worthwhile looking at the practice of advertising.

You have carried out some form of research and now you are in a position where you wish to bring to people's attention your product. Obviously different media are more suited to some businesses than others.

Marketing covers a whole range of activities designed to "identify, anticipate, and satisfy customer needs at a profit" (Chartered Institute of Marketing).

- When do customers want needs satisfied Three questions need to be looked at:
- How do the customers want the need fulfilled
- How much are the customers prepared to pay for that fulfilment

Having found the answers to those questions we have to decide how best to communicate to the target market our ability to meet their needs at a price that they can afford-and communicate that ability to them at a price that we can afford.

There are various options that we can consider. However, some of these options are expensive and may well not be within our reach.

Advertising

Advertising takes various forms. It is exceedingly difficult, unless you have deep pockets, to try to deduce the real effectiveness of whichever form of advertising you decide to employ. For example, is it cost effective to spend £800 on a small advert in a tabloid for one day if that £800 could be spent on something longer lasting.

Advertising hoardings and posters are one way. These tend to cover not only billboards but also tubes trains and buses. Hoardings are seen repeatedly by a wide and ever changing audience in the locality of your choice. They are usually inexpensive.

Leaflets

Leaflets can be distributed on a door-to-door basis (either to other businesses or to individual residences) or they can be given to individuals in the street. However, leaflets can also be thrown away as many see them as junk mail. The result is that leaflets tend to have a low strike rate. Leaflets can also be delivered as inserts in magazines and newspapers. Magazines direct leaflets to specific audiences and newspapers to local areas. Both can prove expensive and again will be discarded more often than not.

A more effective use of leaflets is to have them available in places where the target market will see them. The classic case here is for businesses offering non-residential facilities for holidaymakers. These can usually be found in hotels and guesthouses.

Another use of the leaflet is that of a poster in a newsagent or on other notice boards. This can be effective when being used to attract a defined group of the population who gather together in one place where leaflets cannot be made available. Universities or schools might be a good example.

Directories

Directories will fall into two categories-local and trade. Local directories such as yellow pages are well known mediums of advertising and they are reasonably priced, sometimes free. However, the effectiveness of such advertising depends on what you are doing and also where the ad is placed. Some businesses tend towards directories such as Thompsons because they have less advertisers and are cheaper.

Trade directories are different by their nature. They are unlikely to benefit new businesses as they can be expensive and are in some cases, nationally distributed.

This is of little use if your business is local, of more use if your product is distributed nationally. There are now a number of local area and regional directories, often produced by trade associations. Some are available as a book or on disc for use with computers. Those who subscribe to the disc system often receive monthly or quarterly updates.

Advertising in magazines

Magazines fall into three categories-general national, local or specialist. Magazines tend to be more expensive to advertise in than newspapers but can be more effective. Magazines have a longer life expectancy than newspapers and are often passed on to other readers. Specialist magazines are read by specific people who may form part of your desired target audiences. It is worthwhile bearing in mind that most magazine are national.

Newspaper advertising

National newspapers can obviously reach a lot of people but also tend to be expensive. They are also of little value to those offering local services. Local newspaper advertising can be more effective and also cheaper. Free newspapers are cheaper but can be less effective as they also tend to be seen as junk mail.

Television advertising

It is highly unlikely that television advertising will be relevant in the early years of a business. To launch a television advertising campaign is very expensive indeed. Therefore, this medium will only be a consideration later on, if at all.

Radio advertising

This form of advertising would only be effective if there are sufficient numbers of listeners in the target market. However, in the right circumstances it can be useful and relatively inexpensive. Timing is very important in this medium as you need to target your slots at the most appropriate times and on the most appropriate programme for your intended target audience.

Using an advertising agent

Whether or not an advertising agency is employed will be a matter for the individual business concerned. This decision is down to cost. All businesses placing advertising should set an advertising budget. It could be that placing part of your budget with an agent proves far more cost effective than designing your own campaign. Agents are usually good at designing and placing adverts and can negotiate discounts with various media.

It is certainly worthwhile consulting an agent in order to get an idea of what they can do for you, at the same time raising your own awareness of the direction you should be taking.

Direct mail

Direct mail falls into two categories: untargeted or blanket mailing or targeted. Targeted mail is usually far more effective as untargeted mail can be very expensive and also wasteful. Existing customers of a business are well defined and easily targeted. The secret with direct mail is to keep it short, simple and do it as often as is necessary.

Using sales representatives or agents

Whether or not you choose to use representatives or agents will depend on a number of factors. Where there are few sales required and the selling of a good is complex there may be the need for a representative. Where the product is simple and can be described in an advertisement or leaflet it is unlikely to be necessary to use a representative. There are two main types of representation, the representative or agent.

The representative is a paid member of staff who may or may not receive a bonus or commission based on results. All the representatives running costs will be borne by the business. An agent is a freelance who meets his or her own costs and is paid only on results.

The advantage of using the representative is that he or she uses their entire time devoted to your business and is under your total control.

The agent costs little to run. However, he or she is not totally dedicated to your business. If other products are easier to sell he may ignore yours altogether.

As you can see, there are a number of ways to reach your target audience, once that target audience has been defined. A lot of thought needs to be given to market research and marketing. All too often, they are the first areas to go through the window in search of savings or simply because you are too busy. However, well defined marketing can produce corresponding increase in profits and a clear strategy is an essential part of any business plan.

Internet Marketing

Having looked at more traditional ways of advertising a business, all of which are relevant, it is now time to look at the process of Internet marketing.

Each business has its own overall budget and also goals and targets. In the ideal world it would be nice to be able to invest in both offline and online marketing. However, the reality for most businesses, particularly start-ups, is that funds are limited. In this case, it is crucial to understand the techniques used in online marketing.

Search engine optimization

Most users of the internet will begin the buying process with a search engine. Search engines are enormously powerful and therefore it is essential that your website is built, maintained and updated to be both customer and search engine friendly. Effective search engine optimization is about making your website visible to the search engines, primarily Google.

Making your site visible to search engines

Your site has to be seen to be ranked. Google uses software called Googlebot to scan individual web pages on the internet and what it finds has a direct impact on how thoroughly your site is indexed and how it can rank in the natural Search Engine Results Pages (SERPS).

Quality content

Good content is the key to a good website. Good content will sell your product. Good content will mean that more and more users will visit your site and become consumers of your products and services. In addition, if you have good content then other websites will want to link up to your site therefore increasing the flow of traffic. If your site and its content is seen as good by Google then it will be ranked higher. People looking for a specific good or service will go straight to your site, bypassing the competition. However, in order to ensure that this is the case, your site should be well designed and regularly maintained and updated.

A by-product of creating good content on your website is that other websites will want to link to your content. This can only be good because it puts your website in a position of being an authority on your given product or service. It will result in more traffic to your site and will attract the attention of Google, improving your rankings. It is no good developing a site which looks attractive and then not maintaining it or trying to optimize your rankings. This will set you back and if you are relying more on people finding your site, as opposed to the more traditional forms of marketing, then it is essential to have an ongoing plan for updating and promoting your site.

The use of key words and phrases

You will want to find your main, or niche, keywords and concentrate on writing content to exploit the words. Keywords are the tool through which those who search the web find your unique product. If you are selling bathrooms for example you will want to come up with as many associated words as possible such as 'designer bathrooms' or 'Victorian bathrooms' in other words try to differentiate and provide as many entries as possible for the user. To just use the word 'bathroom' will severely limit the access to your own site.

Search engine marketing

SEM, Paid Search or PPC advertising is a broad subject that will require research on your part to ensure that you know what you are doing before you invest heavily.

SEM allows you to display an advert on the Search Engine Results Pages or the Search Engines network of publisher websites which you can target to display only to users searching for specific keywords or phrases related to your business. You control your account totally, from the text or images of the advert to how much you wish to spend.

If you elect to run PPC adverts with Google, then your ads will be displayed above and to the right of the organic or natural search results, i.e. the sponsored area. Google calls its program Adwords, which is where the search engine makes most of its profits. There are a number of reasons why search engine marketing is effective:

- It is quick to get started
- You are in control of what you spend
- Your campaigns give you instant visibility

What Google has done with Adwords is to create an online auction for every keyword and phrase in every language. The more competitive a keyword, the higher the price. This is how Google makes its money. You should start your Adwords campaign with a small budget, dip your toe in the water, to see how you go. Setting up an account is simple enough and you should ensure that you read the help and FAQ's on the site before committing yourself.

Adwords works by charging you a fee every time someone clicks on your advert-the more you are willing to pay in comparison to others bidding for the same keywords and the better your landing page is (Quality Score) the higher up the sponsored links you will be placed. The bigger your budget, the more users will be shown your advert and the more that will click through. As soon as your budget has been spent, your advert is taken off until the next day. This allows you to keep tight control of your marketing spend and allows you to see very quickly if the campaign is working and to measure the return on your investment.

Purchasing traffic

When you enter into Google Adwords or place a banner ad on another website you are in effect buying traffic to your site. There are some unscrupulous companies around that charge you for delivering visitors to your site and then don't deliver.

Legitimate performance marketing companies do exist and they are well aware of the business need for traffic. They are also quite sophisticated and can direct the right sort of traffic to your site. Performance marketing companies invest heavily in building up their own network of users or publisher's websites which they then exploit by showing their advertiser's (your) sales message to their network. By carefully categorizing and segmenting their user base, they can effectively ensure that your pages are shown to relevant users. If someone wants law books for example they will only show your advertisement to those interested in law books.

Depending on the size and nature of the performance marketing company you can specify the countries in which you want your advert to be shown or even the approximate age or gender of the target audience. The more specific your requirements the more you will be charged for the service. However, because it is performance based, you will only pay when the campaign results in a conversion. The following are a sample of companies that offer Performance marketing.

Burst www.burstmedia.com
DoubleClick www.doubleclick.com
www.conversantmedia.com

And there are many more!

Email marketing

Email marketing is an effective way to send your message before you have had a chance of building up your own database of customers. Performance marketing companies will provide lists that are segmented by interest. You will need to check with the provider that all addresses have been cleared and have given their consent to receive third party promotional emails. I receive many such emails every day which I have not consented to and which I delete, so it is important to do your homework beforehand.

Affiliation (as advertiser)

There are a wide variety of affiliation networks available which marry advertisers to publishers. Most networks charge new advertisers a set-up fee which gives your business access to the network of affiliates. Set-up fees can be hefty so you need to go into this with care. In addition, most networks charge advertisers a monthly fee which covers continued access to the network. Ongoing performance can be monitored through the networks portal and affiliates reports can be generated. The strongest aspect of affiliation is payment on performance. You only pay a commission if your affiliate delivers a lead, registration or sale. You are free to pay as much or as little as you want for each of these conversions. Affiliates take campaigns seriously and invest time, money and effort to promote advertiser's products and services. The relationship is two way and you also have to be serious, keeping them up to date with new products, pricing and any offers or promotions that you intend to run. As with all aspects of business, good communication is the key.

Using vouchers and coupons

The use of vouchers and coupons to promote and sell products, usually at a discount, is becoming increasingly popular with online business. The idea has been around for ever, being used for all sorts of offline business but it is now being used for online trading.

Coupons usually allow customers, whether existing or new, to benefit from a promotion by entering a code online at the point of purchasing. The utilization of the code will modify the customers order in some way corresponding to the offer.

These coupons can be printed and distributed through print media, handed out in the street as a flyer or as part of promotional literature, or through any other medium. they can also be distributed online by adding the coupon to a social media post such as facebook or twitter. They can also be sent to existing customers in a mailshot.

The use of coupons as part of your selling strategy will require some work to your site and again this is what you will be asking your web designer to do for you.

Co-registration

Co-registration is a lead and customer acquisition strategy used by numerous brands. It is performance based-you only pay on results. Co-registration involves placing a short text or image advertisement for your company on the registration pages of high volume third party websites or landing pages. Usually, you are sharing the page with other advertisers who sell similar products or services, or the page is themed in such a way as to link the advertisers. This method of promotion allows users to request additional information about your product or service and in turn provides you with their contact details.

Co-registration allows you to build a permission based, targeted database of consumers interested in your service and, depending on the volume of the third party site, allows you to develop lists very quickly.

Rich media

Rich media is, basically, videos, pod casts and other images which will serve to improve your visibility and differentiate you from other sites selling similar products. Most shop windows have excellent displays and lure customers in. Web portals should be the same and a short video can do wonders when it comes to displaying your product, or telling customers more about you and your company and what products or services you sell.

Social media

Social media, such as Facebook and Twitter is now so widespread that it would be foolish not to advertise your existence on their sites. By opening accounts with platforms such as Facebook, Twitter and Linked In you will be able to reach your potential audience and also hear what is being said about your company, product or service.

Blogging

Adding a blog to your business website is a simple procedure for any web developer and the quality and customization options from the big payers such as Wordspace and Blogger leaves very little need to develop your own platform.

A blog will allow you to produce articles, presenting news and comment about your business and its operations. Blogging helps to develop brand building and may provide you with competitive advantage..

Market places

Market places such as Ebay can be very useful. Although initially conceived as a site where individuals can buy and sell, it now has a facility for professional sellers. Ebay and Amazon in the UK, and Priceminister and Play in Europe, among a few others, provide online business the opportunity to enjoy a worldwide audience by listing your products or services and offering them to their enormous customer base. By paying a listing fee, or a monthly fee plus a share or percentage of the sale price, your business can gain enormous reach within a very short time.

To make it easy for businesses to sell via marketplace sites, these online sellers offer a route to professional sellers to be able to bulk load their products. This is achieved through XML, CSV or through an online portal. There will be some work involved on your side adapting your product database to the platforms particular product classification rules, but once that is done, it is usually a straightforward process loading your products.

The listing fee, commission on sale and other fees can tend to be high if you are selling low margin items. However, the sheer size of the audience can make it worthwhile. As with many other things, it is a case of trying it, dipping your toe in the water and see whether it is worth carrying on.

Now read a summary of the main points from Chapter 11 overleaf.

....

Main points from Chapter 11
Marketing

- Sales are vital to any business. You must be satisfied that there is a demand for your proposed products and you must be able to determine how you can investigate the market in which you want to operate, how many potential clients there are in either the catchment area you operate in or the wider area.
- The tool that is used to determine demand for a product is market research. Market research can be cheap and simple or highly complex depending on how you approach it and what you might want to find out.
- Having carried out market research, you now need to decide on the medium that you will use to advertise. Obviously this will also depend on your franchise and the support that you get from the franchisor.

....

Chapter 12

Growing Your Franchise-A Few Tips

In the previous three chapters, we have looked at the main areas relating to successful business management that you will need to be aware of: financial management; products markets and pricing and finally marketing. Don't forget customer satisfaction! At the end of the whole process of looking for your franchise, financing and getting it going, it will be time to look at the process of developing your business.

When you are actually up and running you may encounter other problems as you go along, such as staff management (if you have staff) and also developing a relationship with the franchisor.

Building a franchise business, like many other businesses, is a delicate balance where you need to grow turnover, for your own profit but at the same time follow the rules set by your franchisor and ensure that you meet their targets.

Most franchise agreements have a fixed initial period, such as five years, which allow you to grow and get used to a particular business and relationships which would not exist if you had started on your own. One of the first areas which we will look at is that of staff management, which could be difficult in the initial period.

Managing staff
Given that your staff are your most important resource, then it is vital that you get the management right. In retail franchises turnover of staff is high, which can be disruptive

which is why you will need to understand the qualities needed to be a good manager, effective leadership qualities. In short, you will need to develop a management style that works. If you are not used to managing people, things can go wrong as sometimes people new to staff management can develop styles that are authoritarian and abrasive and demoralise staff. Others go the opposite way and try too hard to be friendly and accommodating and end up losing respect. To run a motivated and disciplined workforce you need to strike a balance between the two approaches. Depending on the franchisor you will have advice and guidance in terms of training and managing employees and also monitoring their progress.

In addition to actual staff management, you will need to understand and keep abreast of the many rules and regulations that accompany HR and also understand taxation and also pension legislation. Again, your franchisor will help and assist in this area. In fact, depending on the size and nature of the business you are entering into, these are questions that should be asked at the outset before signing any agreement.

Networking
There will be people who are operating with the same franchisor who have been through the hoops. you should make contact with these franchisees and share experiences with them and ask advice. Don't be afraid to do this. The fact that you will be operating in a different territory from them will remove the element of competition and secrecy.

Knowing yourself
In the middle of everything, you need to know your own capabilities. One of the most important things if you are

employing staff is to learn to delegate and not try to keep control of everything yourself, which is a great temptation to begin with. In fact, one shortcoming of many managers in many industries is the lack of ability to delegate. This can and does backfire as staff feel that they are not trusted and cannot develop their own roles effectively.

You need to ensure that you are developing your own knowledge and skills as you go to ensure that you are keeping your business at the forefront and maximising its potential. Running a franchise, as with any other business, requires you to be multi-skilled. There are many roles that you will need to undertake: manager and mentor, financier and accountant, business planner and customer services manager. There are many things that you will be involved in and you should be at least familiar with what they entail, if not an expert. And again, if you recognise that one of your staff has skills in a particular area and enjoys that role, give them their head, so to speak and don't be afraid to let them get on with it.

Managing time

One of the most important elements to being a successful business manager is the ability to manage time. If you can't manage time you will not succeed as there will be so many demands on you that you need to be disciplined and keep all of the balls afloat.

The most important aspect of time management is to ensure that you have listed and prioritised everything that you need to do. Keep a diary, electronic preferably, and refer to it. Don't keep things in your head. You will need long and short term goals outlined . Long term goals will be things such as growing turnover and expanding your customer base. Shorter term goals will be monthly lists, such as setting sales targets, trying new suppliers and dealing with accounts.

The essence of good and effective time management is to make sure that you have clearly outlined plans that you regularly refer to and keep to. In this way you will control time, not the other way round. You will also need to manage your day-to-day time and make sure that essential tasks are dealt with, such as dealing with emails and customer complaints. make sure that you set a regular amount of time aside each day to achieve this. There seems to be 12 universal principles underpinning effective time management and these are listed below:

- Determine what is urgent

Know what to give your time to and what not-don't get bogged down with unnecessary tasks.

- Don't over commit

You might be someone who says yes to everything-it is now important to only commit yourself to things that can realistically be accomplished.

- Have a plan for your time

We have discussed this above, make sure that what you do follows a plan, which has been put together to ensure that the goals and objectives of your business are accomplished.

- Allow time for the unexpected

It is a given that, in the middle of your ideal world, the unexpected will happen. You should acknowledge this and allow yourself some 'slack' in the day which is there to deal with unexpected events.

- Handle things once

Make sure that when you do something, do it once and do it effectively so you don't need to waste time returning to it. A prime example is the answering of emails-make sure that they are read and understood and dealt with the first time round.

- Create realistic deadlines

Make sure that the deadlines that you have set yourself and others are realistic and achievable.

- Set goals for yourself and time

Also touched on above, setting goals should underpin everything that you do within the framework of running your business.

- Develop routines

When used effectively, routines within a working day are a central part of time management. Doing certain things at the same time every day such as opening mail or answering emails. Staff will understand and know that certain things will take place at certain times each day.

- Focus on one thing at a time

If you focus on one task at a time then you will achieve the desired outcome easier than you would if you were multi-tasking. Basically, don't try to do too much at once.

- Eliminate or minimise distractions

You will face distractions wherever you work, whether at home or in an office. You can manage your time so as to either eliminate them or to at least minimise them. Make sure that you have quality time, close the office door at certain times to ensure that you can get things done. get to work early or stay late to accomplish certain things that can be done in quieter times.

- Outsource task or delegate

We touched on the importance of delegation above. make sure that whatever can be delegated is delegated. Don't try and hold on to everything yourself as this is poor time management and poor management overall. If their are tasks that can be outsourced, such as payroll management do so. Don't try to do everything just to save money and in the end you will end up wasting money and time by not doing other things.

- Leave time for fun and play

Finally, don't let your business take over your life. I know very well, from personal experience, that this is easier said than done, especially in the early stages of a business. However, if you let a business consume all of your time then you will burn out and this can have many unfortunate consequences.

This is the main reason for **effective time management**-making sure that you have everything under control within a working day and also in the longer term, so you can release time to be with yourself, family and friends.

****

Summary of this book

As you will have discovered by now, the process of buying and running a successful franchise is complex. The skills needed to run a business generally are numerous. However, for those who get it right the rewards can be numerous. Not only financial but also socially and personally.

To recap:

> ➤ We looked at the nature of franchising generally, what exactly is a franchise. We also looked at the role of the British Franchise Association in providing some sort of regulation and support in an otherwise unregulated industry.
> ➤ We looked at how you go about finding a franchise-the various mediums through which you can identify the business for you. We also looked at the pro's and con's of running a franchise.
> ➤ We looked at the process of raising finance to buy a franchise and the attitude of the banks to lending money.
> ➤ We looked at the nature and importance of the legal agreement that is entered into when buying a franchise.
> ➤ We looked at the nature of the operations manual that (should) set down the ground rules when running a franchise.
> ➤ We looked at the importance of the business skills needed to run a franchise.

This book hasn't been about offering glossy success stories or providing case studies. It is about putting forward the basic essentials that you need to know when buying a franchise, or before entering into a franchise agreement. It is here to ensure that before you become a franchisee you are aware of the basic ground rules. Above all, make sure that the company you are buying from is, in some form or other, a member of the British Franchise association, so that they are subject to some form of regulation.

Good luck with your venture.

****

Franchise glossary of terms

Below is an extensive list of common franchise terms and their definitions.

Advertising Fee – A contribution made to an advertising fund that the franchisor manages for the franchise system. The franchisor uses the fund for national advertising and marketing, or to attract new franchise owners, but not to target your particular outlet. It's usually less then three percent of the franchisee's annual sales and paid in addition to the royalty fee. Not all franchisors charge advertising fees.

Approved Supplier - Suppliers approved or chosen by a franchise company.

Area Franchisee/Area Developer – Buys the rights from the original franchisor to develop the system in a defined region. An area developer cannot sell franchises.

British Franchise Association (bfa) - The bfa, since 1977, has established an ethical code of conduct for franchisors in the UK and ensures the strict enforcement of this code. Over 300 franchises are members of the bfa and adhere to this code of conduct.

Broker – These are independent professionals who market on behalf of franchisors, selling their franchisees on a fee-paying basis. Potential franchisees must always independently evaluate their chosen franchise.

Business Format Franchising - A license to operate a business using a franchisor's product, service and trademark under certain guidelines for a specified time.

Business Plan – A plan that outlines the objectives of a business and the steps necessary to achieve those objectives. This can include financial projections and the planned steps for expansion. If you are seeking funding from a bank or building society you will often be asked to provide your business plan to secure borrowing.

Company-Owned Outlet - An outlet operating under a franchise company brand, but that is owned by the franchisor as opposed to a franchisee. Company-owned outlets are often used by franchisors to trial new ideas and systems before implementing them across the franchised outlets within the network.

Copyright – The franchisor produces manuals and other documentation to ensure the franchise system is uniform. These are the franchisor's documents and they have copyright over them.

Distributorships - Manufacturers and wholesalers grant permission to businesses and individuals to sell their products. A distributorship is normally not a franchise. However, certain distributorship arrangements may qualify as a franchise, may be licensed or be adjudged a business opportunity requiring disclosure.

Estimated Initial Investment - A detailed listing of all fees and expenses you can expect to incur in starting a franchise. This listing represents the total amount that you would need to pay or get financing for.

Exclusive Territory - As a franchisee you can, with the consent of the franchisor, be given an exclusive area around your operation. This area can be large or small and no other franchisee or company owned business would be allowed to operate there.

Franchise - The rights you acquire to offer specific products or services within a certain location for a declared period of time.

Franchise Agreement - outlines the expectations and requirements of the franchisor and describes their commitment to the franchisee. The Franchise Agreement includes information that covers territorial rights of the franchisee, location requirements, training schedule, fees, general obligations of the franchisee, general obligations of the franchisor, etc.

Franchise Fee - An up-front entry fee, usually payable upon the signing of the contract (franchise agreement) for the right to use the franchisor's name, logo, and business system. Often the franchise fee is also the consideration paid for initial training, site selection, operations manuals, and other help given by the franchisor before the opening of the business.

Franchisee - The operator or owner of a franchise.

Franchise Resale – The process of buying a franchise that is already up and running. Franchisees sell on their franchise for a number of reasons; retirement, another business venture, moving overseas, have made their money etc. Whilst the investment may be higher than buying a new franchise, buying a franchise resale minimises the risk of failure and is operational from day one.

Franchise Type - The franchise type identifies in general the type of work involved in running the franchise. There are five main categories, retail franchises, management franchises, single operator manual, single operator executive and investment.

Franchising - a method of doing business within a given industry that involves at least two parties - the franchisor and the franchisee. The contract binding the two parties is the franchise.

Franchisor - The parent company or person that grants, for a fee and other considerations, the right to use its name and system of business operations.

Home-based franchises - these are franchises that can be run from home from a small office. The franchise investment is usually lower with a home-based franchise.

Initial Investment - The funds needed to initially set up a franchise and begin trading. This amount must cover the franchise fee paid to the franchisor and also includes outlay needed to secure space, purchase products, and cover any other initial set-up costs.

Investment - The franchisee invests a significant amount of money in the franchise such as a hotel. The franchisee in this case will be personally working at arm's length from the franchise and will employ a management team to operate it.

Job Franchise – see Single Operator Manual.

Management Franchise - The franchisee will be using their experience to grow the business and control staff who carry out the tasks of the job. It will require premises, which are more likely to be office than a High Street outlet. The majority of the turnover from management franchises is generated from Business to Business activities rather than from retail.

Management Service Fee - A term for Royalties, usually in the form of a fixed fee or percentage.

Marketing Plan - a marketing plan should form part of your overall business plan. The purpose of the marketing plan is to define your market, i.e. identify your customers and competitors, to outline a strategy for attracting and keeping customers and to identify and anticipate change.

Master Franchisee/License - This is a franchisee who is given the right by the franchisor to develop and sell franchises under the brand name within a certain territory. Unlike area development rights, where a franchisee can open outlets themselves within a given region, a master franchise owner must only sell franchises in a particular region.

Multi-Level Marketing - A form of distributorship in which you receive commission on your own sales and on the sales of others whom you sign up as distributors. Some MLMs are considered pyramid schemes and illegal in some countires. Some are legitimate business opportunities. Any business of this nature should be investigated closely.

Multi-Unit Franchise - The franchisor awards the right to a franchisee to operate more than one unit within a defined area based on an agreed upon development schedule.

Offer - An oral or written proposal to sell a franchise to a prospective franchisee upon understood general terms and conditions.

Operating Manual - Comprehensive guidelines advising a franchisee on how to operate the franchised business. It covers all aspects of the business, and may be separated into different manuals addressing such subjects as accounting, personnel, advertising, promotion and maintenance.

Product Format Franchise – Once the rights to market a product or service have been acquired, you may offer other products along side your "product franchise."

Regional Franchise - Buys the rights from a master franchisee or the original franchisor to sell franchises in a defined region.

Renewal - The rights given to a franchisee to renew their franchise business once the initial period set out in the franchise agreement has lapsed. The franchise agreement should also state the terms and conditions under which both parties agree that the business relationship can or cannot be renewed.

Retail Franchise - The franchise will occupy retail premises, selling products or services during retail hours for 'walk-in' retail. The business is totally dependent on the premises and turnover is achieved from walk-in consumers.

Royalty Fees - Ongoing fees paid to the franchisor by franchisees in respect of ongoing training and support services provided, usually a % of turnover.

Single Operator Executive - (Also referred to as a 'white collar' Job Franchise)- the franchisee will be working at the franchise which usually takes the form of a trade supplying, selling and delivering products or service. It may be mobile, home-based or requiring small office premises. The type of work is executive.

Single Operator Manual (Also referred to as Job Franchise) - the franchisee will be working at the franchise which usually takes the form of a trade supplying, selling and delivering products or service. It may be mobile, home-based or requiring small office premises.

Termination - Refers to the legal provisions by which either party in the relationship may terminate the contract, e.g., for breach of contract.

Territory/Area - That 'exclusive' portion of land, on a national, regional/area, county, metropolitan or postcode basis, which is allocated to franchisees as part of the franchise package.

Total Investment – The amount of money estimated for complete set up of a franchisee's business, including the initial investment, the working capital, and subsequent additions to inventory and equipment deemed necessary for a fully operational and profitable enterprise.

Turnkey Package - A package that includes all the systems, information and equipment a franchisee needs to be able to 'turn the key' and start trading.

Working Capital - Initially funds are needed to pay first and last months rent, utility deposits, licenses and any number of incidental costs. As it takes time to build up a new business the first months are usually loss months, which need to be financed.

****

Useful Addresses and Websites

The British Franchise Association
www.thebfa.org

Finding a franchise
www.franchisedirect.co.uk
www.whichfranchise.co.uk
www.businessesforsale.com/uk/franchises
www.franchises.com

Financing a franchise
www.fundingcircle.com/business loans
www.business.hsbc.co.uk
www.franchisefinance.co.uk
www.startups.co.uk/1/2/franchisebuying-franchise

Legal agreements
www.thebfa.org/members/affiliates/legal-advisors
www.whcihfranchise.com/legaladvisors
www.smallbusiness.co.uk

****

Index

Accountancy, 23
ACORN, 8, 106, 107
Advertising, 5, 9, 13, 63, 111, 121, 122, 142
Advertising fees, 63
Adwords, 127, 128
Affiliation, 9, 129
Amazon, 132
Analysed Cash book System, 8, 101
Automotive, 4, 23, 37

Benefit and lifestyle segmentation, 8, 107
Blogging, 10, 131, 132
British Franchise Association, 11, 12, 13, 61, 142, 150
Burger King, 22
Business, 98
Business Format Franchising, 3, 20, 143
Business Franchise Magazine, 52
Business plan, 57, 72

Cash Flow Model, 64
Cashflow, 8, 96
Cleaning, 4, 24, 40
Cocoa Cola, 22
Coffee, 24
Competitive advantage, 8, 108
Computerised Accounting Systems, 8, 103
Computers, 24
Consulting, 23
Copyright, 2, 75, 143
Co-registration, 9, 130, 131
Coupons, 9, 130
Couriers, 24

Creditors, 97
Daily Express, 52
Dalton's Weekly, 52
Dating, 24
Debtors, 96
Demographic segmentation, 8, 106
Deposits, 61
Direct mail, 124
Directories, 122
Discrimination, 7, 89
Dyno Rod, 22

Ebay, 132
Education, 24
Email marketing, 9, 129
Enterprise Finance Guarantee, 59
Estate Agency, 24

Facebook, 131
Financial Control, 7, 95, 104
Financing a Purchase, 57, 72
Fitness, 24
Food, 24
Franchise Agreement, 6, 73, 84, 144
Franchise agreements, 30
Franchise Fees, 5, 62
Franchise support, 7, 81
Franchise training, 7, 83
Franchise World, 52
Franchisor Monitoring, 4, 30

Gardening, 24
General Motors, 22
Geographic segmentation, 8, 106
Golf, 24

Google, 125, 126, 127, 128
Health, 23, 24, 67
Home Care, 24
Home Improvements, 24
Home Services, 24

Internet, 4, 9, 24, 43, 125
Internet marketing, 125

Key words, 9, 126

Leaflets, 121
Leisure, 24
Loan accounts, 60

Managing staff, 10, 135
Market Research, 117
Marketing, 6, 7, 9, 61, 66, 80, 120, 125, 133, 146
Marketing Plan, 6, 66, 146
McDonalds, 22, 23, 46
Merchandising, 24

National Exhibition Centre, 52
National Insurance, 111
Networking, 10, 136

Occupation and social class, 8, 106
Operations manual, 79

Pepsi Cola, 22
Pest Control, 24
Pets, 24
Photography, 24
Pricing, 7, 9, 81, 105, 110, 115
Product and Trade Name Franchising, 3, 21

Product segmentation, 8, 107
Profit and loss, 8, 95
Profit Forecast, 64
Property, 6, 24, 75
Proprietary systems, 8, 100

Recruiting staff, 6, 7, 80, 88
Recruitment, 4, 14, 24, 45, 61
Retail, 4, 24, 46, 147
Rich media, 9, 131

Sales, 99
Search engine, 9, 125, 127
Search engine optimization, 9, 125
Search Engine Results Pages, 125, 127
Segmenting the market place, 8, 105
Senior Care, 23
Service Charges, 30
Service Marks, 6, 75
Social, 9, 131
Sport, 24
Stock, 97
Subway, 23, 46, 87
SWOT analysis, 108
System Double Entry, 8, 102

Tax, 99, 100
Television advertising, 9, 123
The British and International Franchise Exhibition and, 52
The Franchise Magazine, 52
Trade Marks, 6, 75
Travel, 24
Twitter, 131

Unethical franchisors, 4, 32

Unique selling points (USP), 9, 109
VAT, 99, 100, 102
Vending, 24
Vouchers, 9, 130

Wedding Planning, 24
What Franchise Magazine, 52

....

www.straightforwardco.co.uk

All titles, listed below, in the Straightforward Guides Series can be purchased online, using credit card or other forms of payment by going to www.straightfowardco.co.uk A discount of 25% per title is offered with online purchases.

Law

A Straightforward Guide to:
Consumer Rights
Bankruptcy Insolvency and the Law
Employment Law
Private Tenants Rights
Family law
Small Claims in the County Court
Contract law
Intellectual Property and the law
Divorce and the law
Leaseholders Rights
The Process of Conveyancing
Knowing Your Rights and Using the Courts
Producing Your own Will
Housing Rights
The Bailiff the law and You
Probate and The Law
Company law
What to Expect When You Go to Court
Give me Your Money-Guide to Effective Debt Collection
Caring for a Disabled Child

General titles

Letting Property for Profit
Buying, Selling and Renting property

Buying a Home in England and France
Bookkeeping and Accounts for Small Business
Creative Writing
Freelance Writing
Writing Your own Life Story
Writing performance Poetry
Writing Romantic Fiction
Speech Writing
Teaching Your Child to Swim
Creating a Successful Commercial Website
The Straightforward Business Plan
The Straightforward C.V.
Successful Public Speaking
Handling Bereavement
Play the Game-A Compendium of Rules
Individual and Personal Finance
Understanding Mental Illness
The Two Minute Message
Guide to Self Defence
Tiling for Beginners

Go to:

www.straightforwardco.co.uk